Other Books

by

FRED REINFELD

CHESS MASTERY
BY QUESTION AND ANSWER

CHESS FOR AMATEURS
How to Improve Your Game

PRACTICAL END-GAME PLAY

KERES' BEST GAMES OF CHESS

TARRASCH'S
BEST GAMES OF CHESS

THE IMMORTAL GAMES
OF CAPABLANCA

CHESS BY YOURSELF

BOTVINNIK THE INVINCIBLE

CHESS STRATEGY AND TACTICS
With Irving Chernev

LEARN CHESS FAST
with Sammy Reshevsky

NIMZOVICH THE HYPERMODERN

LEARN CHESS FROM THE MASTERS

THE ART OF CHESS

HOW TO FORCE CHECKMATE

WIN AT CHESS

FRED REINFELD

HOW TO
FORCE CHECKMATE

(Formerly titled Challenge to Chessplayers)

dover publications inc new york · new york

This new Dover edition first published in 1958,
is an unabridged and unaltered republication
of the work formerly published under the title
Challenge to Chessplayers.

Library of Congress Catalog Card Number: 57-14881

Manufactured in the United States of America

Dover Publications, Inc.
180 Varick Street
New York, N. Y. 10014

Contents

HOW TO
FORCE CHECKMATE

Mate on the Move

IN RECENT YEARS we have had a great many fine books on chess, dealing with almost every conceivable aspect of the game. Yet these books have neglected what is after all the primary object of a game of chess: *the actual process of checkmating your opponent's King.* The purpose of this book is to instruct you, the reader, in all the many ways of achieving checkmate. Another and equally important aim is to give you the pleasant and entertaining task of solving three hundred carefully selected positions. This is a continuation of the "learn by doing" technique which has been applied successfully in *Chess Mastery By Question and Answer, Chess for Amateurs, Chess Quiz* and *Chess By Yourself.*

We begin with the task which is not only the most fundamental one, but also the easiest: mate on the move. These fairly simple positions will train your batting eye, as it were; they will give you a flair for the quickly decisive move. They are not always easy, so be on your guard for quirks, finesses and optical illusions!

MATE ON THE MOVE

DIAGRAM 1
White moves
Black: AMATEUR

White: ROSENTHAL

188?

DIAGRAM 2
White moves
Black: WOLLNER

White: CHAROUSEK

Kassa, 1893

DIAGRAM 3
Black moves
Black: ANDERSSEN

White: ROSANES

Breslau, 1863

DIAGRAM 4
Black moves
Black: ZUKERTORT

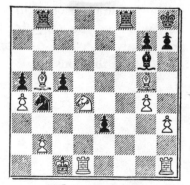

White: ALLIES

Chislehurst, 1878

DIAGRAM 5
White moves
Black: LEELAUS

White: NIMZOVICH
Riga, 1912

DIAGRAM 6
Black moves
Black: MAROCZY

White: ALBIN
Monte Carlo, 1903

1. 1 B—Kt6 *mate*. Note the criss-cross action of White's Bishops.

2. 1 B x QP *mate*. Only double check does the trick.

3. 1 . . . R—K8 *mate*. Conclusion of a fine combination.

4. 1 . . . Kt—R7 *mate*. Zukertort played this game blindfold, and one of his opponents was Louis Bonaparte.

5. 1 B—B5 *mate*. Conclusion of a game in which Nimzovich gave the odds of Queen!

6. 1 . . . Q—R4 *mate*. See what a vast difference there is between rigorous tournament play and carefree skittles chess! Most players would be more than happy to win "only" the Queen with *1* . . . Kt x Q; but Black goes straight for the mate.

9

MATE ON THE MOVE

DIAGRAM 7
White moves
Black: ZUKERTORT

White: BLACKBURNE
London, 1881

DIAGRAM 8
White moves
Black: TINSLEY

White: TEICHMANN
Hastings, 1895

DIAGRAM 9
White moves
Black: SENATOR

White: ZUKERTORT
Posen, 1867

DIAGRAM 10
Black moves
Black: TARRASCH

White: AMATEUR
Munich, 1915

SOLUTIONS

DIAGRAM 11
White moves
Black: AMATEUR

White: HOFFER
London, 1880

DIAGRAM 12
White moves
Black: HOLM

White: SUNDERSTROM
Stockholm, 1912

7. *1* Kt—Q7 *mate*. In cases of discovered check, it is literally true that "the hand is quicker than the eye."

8. *1* Q—R6 *mate*. This one looks like an optical illusion!

9. *1* Kt—K6 *mate*. The sequel to a Queen sacrifice.

10. *1 . . .* B—B6 *mate*. Tarrasch prepared this position with a series of judicious sacrifices. The Bishops are brutal in such situations!

11. *1* Kt—B7 *mate*. This was the point of an earlier Queen sacrifice.

12. *1* Kt x P *mate*. How did Black's King stray so far from home?!

11

MATE ON THE MOVE

DIAGRAM 13
Black moves
Black: THOMAS

White: AMATEUR
Quincy, 1945

DIAGRAM 14
White moves
Black: LABOURDONNAIS

White: McDONNELL
Match, 1834

DIAGRAM 15
Black moves
Black: UEDEMAN

White: JANICE
St. Louis, 1902

DIAGRAM 16
White moves
Black: KLEIN

White: DENKER
Washington, D. C., 1945

DIAGRAM 17
Black moves
Black: GILBERT

White: MURRAY
Minnesota Championship,
1946

DIAGRAM 18
Black moves
Black: JOHNER

White: SPIELMANN
Vienna, 1908

13. 1 . . . Kt—B6 mate. This game took all of five moves.

14. 1 B—B4 mate. Such conclusions have become obsolete in World Championship play.

15. 1 . . . P—B8(Kt) mate. Successful underpromotion is so rare in practical chess that it always makes a charming impression.

16. 1 Q—Kt7 mate. The Black Queen's protection was only a sham.

17. 1 . . . Kt—Kt6 mate. It comes as a surprise to see Black's Bishop lurking coyly in the background at QR2.

18. 1 . . . B—Q6 mate. In this example the Bishops are again in full command of the board.

MATE ON THE MOVE

DIAGRAM 19
Black moves
Black: PARR

White: MULDER
Anglo-Dutch Match, 1939

DIAGRAM 20
Black moves
Black: NIMZOVICH

White: ALLIES
Zurich, 1905

DIAGRAM 21
Black moves
Black: RADSPINNER

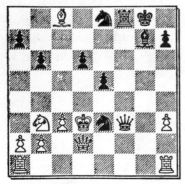

White: KAGAN
Boston, 1946

DIAGRAM 22
Black moves
Black: TARRASCH

White: AMATEUR
Munich, 1923

DIAGRAM 23
Black moves
Black: CAPABLANCA

White: CORIA
Buenos Aires, 1914

DIAGRAM 24
White moves
Black: SHAYNE

White: DENKER
Rochester, 1945

19. *1 . . . Kt—R6 mate.* Neglected development on the part of White.

20. *1 . . . Kt—Q6 mate.* Nimzovich gave Queen odds in this game.

21. *1 . . . P—K5 mate.* A case of well-deserved punishment. White's King was out of bounds.

22. *1 . . . Kt—Kt8 mate.* An unconventional follow-up to a Queen sacrifice.

23. *1 . . . Kt—R6 mate.* A good example of the destructive effect of a broken-up Pawn position in front of the castled King.

24. *1 Kt—Q6 mate.* This unusual smothered mate resulted from Black's greed for material and delay in development.

15

MATE ON THE MOVE

DIAGRAM 25
Black moves
Black: DZAGUROV

White: OSMOLOVSKY
USSR, 1939

DIAGRAM 26
White moves
Black: ALONSO

White: KOLTANOWSKI
Havana, 1946

DIAGRAM 27
Black moves
Black: SCHLECHTER

White: FRIED
Vienna, 1897

DIAGRAM 28
White moves
Black: ILIESCO

White: LETELIER
Buenos Aires, 1945

DIAGRAM 29
White moves
Black: ROMIH

White: NIMZOVICH
Match, 1927

DIAGRAM 30
Black moves
Black: WOOD

White: FRIEDMANN
London Championship, 1945

25. *1 . . . Kt—B6 mate.* The White Queen-side pieces are not functioning.

26. *1 Q x P mate.* White's Bishops are all-powerful.

27. *1 . . . P—B4 mate.* Another Queen sacrifice has paid off.

28. *1 Q—R3 mate.* Black, with a piece down, was lost in any event.

29. *1 Q—B6 mate.* A very instructive situation: Black's considerable material advantage is nullified by the fatal exposure of his King.

30. *1 . . . Kt x Q mate.* Quite a move: Black wins the Queen and simultaneously mates.

MATE ON THE MOVE

DIAGRAM 31
White moves
Black: DUFRESNE

White: KOSSAK
Berlin, 1851

DIAGRAM 32
White moves
Black: KMOCH

White: TARTAKOVER
Niendorf, 1927

DIAGRAM 33
Black moves
Black: MORPHY

White: MARACHE
New York, 1857

DIAGRAM 34
Black moves
Black: MUND

White: TCHIGORIN
Lodz, 1904

DIAGRAM 35
White moves
Black: RYCKHOFF

White: NIMZOVICH
Pernau, 1910

DIAGRAM 36
Black moves
Black: KOSTICH

White: MUEHLOCK
Cologne, 1912

SOLUTIONS

31. 1 Kt—K7 *mate.* An amusing tableau.

32. 1 Q—Kt7 *mate.* The Bishop functions craftily behind the scenes.

33. 1 . . . Kt(5)—K7 *mate.* The great Morphy naturally prefers this to the banal recapture of the Queen.

34. 1 . . . Kt—B5 *mate.* This came after a Queen sacrifice. From one of Tchigorin's simultaneous exhibitions.

35. 1 B—Kt5 *mate.* A remarkable demonstration of the power of a double check.

36. 1 . . . Kt—B6 *mate.* An unusual kind of smothered mate.

Mate in Two Moves

THE PROBLEMS in the previous section were quite simple, were they not? Now we come to more difficult tasks. So far we have dealt with artless "one-liners" with a direct, clean-cut theme; but at this point we enter the realm of combination.

We may define the magic word combination in two different ways: as a series of moves having a common object, or as the blending of objective with method.

Take the first definition: we have to accomplish our task in a given number of moves, and they cannot be any old moves. No indeed; they must be purposeful, calculated, precise, and they must be *linked by the same idea.* The first move will provide the setting, the second move will provide the execution (you may take this as a pun!).

As for the second definition: our objective (checkmating the hostile King) guides us in our choice of moves. We will find the right moves only if we know what we are looking for. Thus these problems serve a useful purpose in training us how to discern our goals, and how to achieve them.

MATE IN TWO MOVES

DIAGRAM 37
White moves
Black: STUBENRAUCH

White: SCHLECHTER

Staffelstein, 1901

DIAGRAM 38
White moves
Black: L'HERMET

White: SPIELMANN

Magdeburg, 1927

DIAGRAM 39
White moves
Black: WYVILL

White: ANDERSSEN

London, 1851

DIAGRAM 40
White moves
Black: PILLSBURY

White: MARSHALL

Vienna, 1903

DIAGRAM 41
White moves
Black: ALAPIN

White: NIMZOVICH
Riga, 1913

DIAGRAM 42
White moves
Black: DUHM

White: PESTALOZZI
Berne, 1908

37. *1* Q—R7*ch*, K—Kt5; *2* Q—R3 *mate*. Another way is *1* P—Kt4*ch*, K x P; *2* Q—R3 *mate*.

38. *1* P—R7*ch*, K—B1; *2* P—R8 (Q) *mate*. White also mates by promoting to a Rook. Sequel to a Queen sacrifice.

39. *1* R—Q8*ch*, R x R; *2* R x R *mate*. Unprotected first rank!

40. *1* P—Q8(Q)*ch*, K—Kt2; *2* Q—R6 *mate*. White can also mate by promoting to a Rook on the first move, or by *2* Q(6)—Q7*ch* or *2* Q(8)—Kt8*ch*. Still another way is *1* Q—B6*ch*, K—Kt1; *2* Q—B8 *mate* or *2* P—Q8(Q) *mate* or *2* P—Q8(R) *mate*.

41. *1* Q—Q8*ch!*, B x Q; *2* R—K8 *mate*. Black's neglected development proved fatal.

42. *1* Q—R8*ch*, K—K2; *2* Q x P *mate*.

MATE IN TWO MOVES

DIAGRAM 43
White moves
Black: SHIPLEY

White: ALBIN
New York, 1894

DIAGRAM 44
Black moves
Black: LOYD

White: FITZGERALD
1898

DIAGRAM 45
Black moves
Black: NEUMANN

White: PAULSEN
Berlin, 1864

DIAGRAM 46
Black moves
Black: GLAESSER

White: BUSH
Postal Game, 1945

DIAGRAM 47
White moves
Black: AMATEUR

White: TCHIGORIN
St. Petersburg, 1894

DIAGRAM 48
White moves
Black: BOGOLYUBOV

White: MARSHALL
New York, 1924

43. *1* Kt—K7*ch*, K—R1; *2* Kt x P *mate*. Windup of a Queen sacrifice.

44. *1* . . . P—B5*ch*; *2* K—B2, Kt—K6 *mate*. Not so easy! This position reminds one of Loyd's ingenious problems and puzzles.

45. *1* . . . R x R*ch*; *2* Kt x R, Q—B8 *mate*. With so much hostile mating force near the White King and with his own pieces dispersed, the mate follows as a matter of course.

46. *1* . . . Kt—R7*ch!* [to make room for the Queen]; *2* B x Kt, Q—Kt5 *mate*.

47. *1* Q—K8*ch*, Kt x Q; *2* R—B8 *mate*. As in the previous example, the first move clears the way.

48. *1* B—Q3*ch*, K x Kt; *2* Q—B2 *mate*. Conclusion of a brilliancy prize game.

25

MATE IN TWO MOVES

DIAGRAM 49
Black moves
Black: SCHLECHTER

White: PETTERSON
Stockholm, 1906

DIAGRAM 50
White moves
Black: Y

White: X

DIAGRAM 51
White moves
Black: ROSENTHAL

White: KOLISCH
Paris, 1864

DIAGRAM 52
White moves
Black: PRICE

White: BLACKBURNE
Birmingham, 1906

DIAGRAM 53
Black moves
Black: PAULSEN

White: V. SCHMIDT
Leipzig, 1864

DIAGRAM 54
White moves
Black: GOSSIP

White: TCHIGORIN
New York, 1889

49. 1 . . . R—R8*ch;* 2 Kt x R, R x Kt *mate.* An unusual kind of finish.

50. 1 R x Kt*ch,* K x R; 2 Q—R5 *mate.* Black castled into a catastrophe. White's pieces are poised for quick action.

51. 1 R—K7*ch,* K—B1; 2 B—K6 *mate.* It is remarkable that the White Queen is superfluous for mating purposes.

52. 1 P—Q4*ch!,* P x P e.p.; 2 Q(4)—B4 *mate.* A pretty finish from a simultaneous exhibition.

53. 1 . . . Q x R*ch;* 2 K x Q, R—B8 *mate.* The White Queen was out of play.

54. 1 B—Kt5*ch,* K x B; 2 Kt —Q6 *mate.* From a tournament game which went all of fifteen moves!

27

MATE IN TWO MOVES

DIAGRAM 55
White moves
Black: AMATEUR

White: BANNET
Cracow, 1897

DIAGRAM 56
Black moves
Black: MALYUTIN

White: NAVRODSKY
St. Petersburg, 1910

DIAGRAM 57
Black moves
Black: GAMBARASHVILLI

White: SEREDA
Tiflis, 1934

DIAGRAM 58
Black moves
Black: TARRASCH

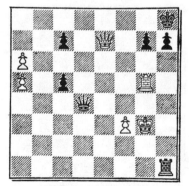

White: MARCO
Hastings, 1895

DIAGRAM 59
Black moves
Black: BLACKBURNE

White: V. ZABERN
Manchester, 1880

DIAGRAM 60
White moves
Black: BOSTWICK

White: JANOWSKI
New York, 1899

55. 1 B—R6*ch*, K x Kt; 2 Q—Kt4 *mate*. Black played badly to arrive at such a position.

56. 1 . . . Kt—K7*ch*; 2 K—B1, Kt x P *mate*. Aftermath of a Queen sacrifice.

57. 1 . . . Kt x P*ch*; 2 Kt x Kt, Kt—Kt6 *mate*. A charmingly unconventional setting for a smothered mate. As a matter of fact, practical examples of this theme rarely follow the orthodox pattern for smothered mate.

58. 1 . . . Q—R5*ch*; 2 K—Kt2, Q—R7 *mate*. White's forces failed to aid the King.

59. 1 . . . R—Kt8*ch!*; 2 B x R, Q—K7 *mate*. Another fine clearance sacrifice.

60. 1 Kt—R6*ch*, K—B1; 2 Kt x P *mate*. Nice work by the Knights.

29

MATE IN TWO MOVES

DIAGRAM 61
Black moves
Black: SALMINGER

White: VARAIN
Munich, 1896

DIAGRAM 62
White moves
Black: ROSENTHAL

White: NEUMANN
Paris, 1867

DIAGRAM 63
Black moves
Black: TCHIGORIN

White: MASON
Paris, 1900

DIAGRAM 64
White moves
Black: WYLDE

White: BLACKBURNE
Manchester, 1875

DIAGRAM 65
White moves
Black: MIESES

White: MAROCZY
Paris, 1900

DIAGRAM 66
White moves
Black: FROEHLICH

White: BERGER
Graz, 1888

61. *1 . . .* Kt—B7*ch; 2* K—Kt1, Kt x P *mate.* Illustrates the fearful power of a double check.

62. *1* Q—B8*ch,* K—K2; *2* R—K6 *mate.* This example shows that the *position* of the pieces is all-important. Despite near-equality of material, Black is helpless.

63. *1 . . .* R—R6*ch; 2* R x R, Q—Kt7 *mate.* Another delightful clearing sacrifice.

64. *1* Q—R7*ch,* Kt x Q; *2* B x Kt *mate.* Hardly surprising, in view of White's concentrated forces on the Kingside.

65. *1* R x B*ch,* K x R; *2* Q—Kt7 *mate.* Black's Queen is out of play.

66. *1* Kt—B6*ch,* P x Kt; *2* B x P *mate.* White had just sacrificed his Queen for a familiar mate pattern.

MATE IN TWO MOVES

DIAGRAM 67
Black moves
Black: PAULSEN

White: BEUTHNER
Leipzig, 1863

DIAGRAM 68
Black moves
Black: BLACKBURNE

White: AMATEUR
Norwich, 1871

DIAGRAM 69
White moves
Black: GRANAS

White: RUBINSTEIN
Lodz, 1905

DIAGRAM 70
White moves
Black: BURN

White: BIRD
London, 1886

DIAGRAM 71
White moves
Black: ALLIES

White: MORPHY
Paris, 1858

DIAGRAM 72
White moves
Black: BARDELEBEN

White: SCHLECHTER
Prague, 1908

67. 1 . . . R x R*ch;* *2* K x R, Q—K8 *mate.* The pin is too much for White.

68. 1 . . . Q—Kt7*ch!;* *2* R x Q, Kt—R6 *mate.* Most artistic.

69. 1 Q—Q5*ch,* K—Kt3; *2* Q—Kt5 *mate.* Another way is *1* Q—K6*ch,* K—B4; *2* B—K7 *mate.*

70. 1 Q x B*ch,* K x Q; *2* B—K2 *mate.* The Black King's last trip.

71. 1 Q—Kt8*ch,* Kt x Q; *2* R—Q8 *mate.* Conclusion of the famous game played at the Paris Opera House during an intermission in the performance of *The Barber of Seville.*

72. 1 R—R5*ch!,* Kt x R; *2* P—Kt5 *mate.* Schlechter was a problem connoisseur.

MATE IN TWO MOVES

DIAGRAM 73
Black moves
Black: GUNSBERG

White: STEINITZ
Match, 1891

DIAGRAM 74
White moves
Black: SHOWALTER

White: BLACKBURNE
New York, 1889

DIAGRAM 75
White moves
Black: SMITH

White: MARCO
London, 1899

DIAGRAM 76
White moves
Black: FORSYTH

White: BLACKBURNE
Edinburgh, 1894

DIAGRAM 77
Black moves
Black: KUCZYNSKY

White: LEWNTON
Lodz, 1905

DIAGRAM 78
White moves
Black: EKSTROM

White: TARTAKOVER
Hastings, 1945–46

73. 1 . . . R—Kt4ch; 2 K— R4, B—B7 mate.

74. 1 Q x KPch, K—B5; 2 Kt —R3 mate. Such a situation is almost unthinkable between first-rate masters.

75. 1 Q x Qch, R x Q; 2 R— Kt8 mate. Very easy, but neat all the same.

76. 1 Q—B8ch, R x Q; 2 Kt —Q7 mate. In the course of a sixty year career, the British master produced many beautiful combinations.

77. 1 . . . Q—Kt6ch!; 2 P x Q, P x P mate. A most unusual finish.

78. 1 R—B8ch, K x R; 2 Q—B7 mate. With a piece ahead, White had an easy win in any event; but the clearance sacrifice was the quickest—and prettiest.

35

MATE IN TWO MOVES

DIAGRAM 79
White moves
Black: MORTIMER

White: KOLISCH

London, 1862

DIAGRAM 80
Black moves
Black: BLEDOW

White: HORWITZ

Berlin, 1837

DIAGRAM 81
White moves
Black: AMATEUR

White: BLACKBURNE

London, 1887

DIAGRAM 82
White moves
Black: AMATEUR

White: ARMSTRONG

Postal Game, 1913

DIAGRAM 83
Black moves
Black: SCHLECHTER

White: MASON
Hastings, 1895

DIAGRAM 84
Black moves
Black: KIESERITZKY

White: SCHULTEN
Paris, 1846

79. *1* Q—B7*ch*, K—Q1; *2* Q—Q7 *mate.* Black's undeveloped Rooks were no match for White's agile Queen.

80. *1* . . . B x P*ch*; *2* K—B1, Kt—Kt6 *mate.* Bledow had just sacrificed the Queen to achieve this amusing finish.

81. *1* R x P*ch*, K x R [or *1* . . . K—R1]; *2* Q x P *mate.* Open lines are decisive.

82. *1* Q x P*ch!*, K x R; *2* R—R5 *mate.* This pleasing mate has been attributed to many sources.

83. *1* . . . R—B7*ch*; *2* K—Q1 [or *2* K—B1], Kt—K6 *mate.* Note the lack of cooperation among the White forces.

84. *1* . . . Kt—B6*ch*; *2* K—R5, B—Kt5 *mate.* Kieseritzky gave up his Queen to force this finish.

MATE IN TWO MOVES

DIAGRAM 85
Black moves
Black: TARRASCH

White: ECKART
Nuremberg, 1889

DIAGRAM 86
Black moves
Black: NAIDORF

White: GLUCKSBERG
Warsaw, 1935

DIAGRAM 87
Black moves
Black: BLACKBURNE

White: HEYERMANS
Rotterdam, 1880

DIAGRAM 88
Black moves
Black: TOLLIT

White: ASHLEY
Birmingham, 1923

DIAGRAM 89
White moves
Black: MATTHEWS

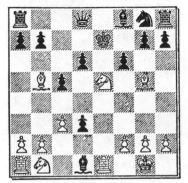

White: POTTER
London, 1868

DIAGRAM 90
White moves
Black: V. BILGUER

White: BLEDOW
Berlin, 1838

85. *1* . . . R—Kt7*ch;* 2 K—Q3, Q—Kt8 *mate.* Economical!

86. *1* . . . Kt—K4*ch;* 2 P x Kt, P—R4 *mate.* Conclusion of a remarkably brilliant game. Known as the "Polish Immortal," the game is perhaps the most brilliant of this century.

87. *1* . . . R—Q8*ch;* 2 B x R [or 2 R x R], P x B(Q) *mate.* Promotion to Rook also does the trick.

88. *1* . . . R x P*ch;* 2 P x R, B—B6 *mate.* The point of the previous Queen sacrifice.

89. *1* Kt—Kt6*ch,* K—B2; 2 Kt x R *mate.* Double checks are nasty!

90. *1* Q—B8*ch,* R x Q; 2 R x R *mate.* Black has played badly.

MATE IN TWO MOVES

DIAGRAM 91
White moves
Black: SCHULTZ

White: LUPRECHT
Postal Game, 1945

DIAGRAM 92
White moves
Black: AMATEUR

White: BLACKBURNE
London, 1886

DIAGRAM 93
White moves
Black: MACDONNELL

White: EVANS
London, 1830

DIAGRAM 94
Black moves
Black: JANNY

White: SCHIFFERS
Budapest, 1898

DIAGRAM 95
Black moves
Black: KEISER

White: COULTER
Postal Game, 1943

DIAGRAM 96
Black moves
Black: BLACKBURNE

White: AMATEUR
London, 1880

91. 1 P—B5*ch,* K—K3; *2* Q—Kt3 *mate.* Once more Queen-side castling has proved insecure.

92. 1 Q—Q5*ch,* Kt x Q; *2* P x Kt *mate.* Black failed to develop properly.

93. 1 Q—K6*ch,* K—B2; *2* B—Q6 *mate.* Black's forces are fatally divided.

94. 1 . . . P—R5*ch; 2* K x Kt, P—Q3 [or *2* . . . P—Q4 *mate*] *mate.* White must have played badly to succumb at such an early stage.

95. 1 . . . Q—R7*ch!; 2* Kt x Q, Kt(8)—Kt6 *mate.* A beautiful blocking sacrifice.

96. 1 . . . Q x P*ch; 2* P x Q, B x P *mate.* Black made wholesale sacrifices to reach this position.

41

MATE IN TWO MOVES

DIAGRAM 97
Black moves
Black: TARRASCH

White: SCHWARTZ
Nuremberg, 1883

DIAGRAM 98
Black moves
Black: TARTAKOVER

White: STEINER
Hastings, 1945–46

DIAGRAM 99
White moves
Black: AMATEUR

White: KOLISCH
London, 1887

DIAGRAM 100
White moves
Black: JOURNOUX

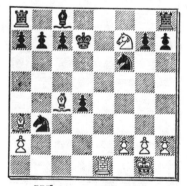

White: DE RIVIERE
Paris, 1860

DIAGRAM 101
Black moves
Black: BOTVINNIK

White: DUBININ
USSR Championship, 1939

DIAGRAM 102
Black moves
Black: TAYLOR

White: CAPON
Thorp, 1873

SOLUTIONS

97. *1 . . . Q x Ktch; 2 K x Q, R—Q8 mate.* A Danish Gambit which backfired!

98. *1 . . . Q—Kt7ch; 2 K x Kt, Q—Kt5 mate* [or *2 . . . R—B1 mate*]. Another way is *1 . . . P—R5ch; 2 K x Kt, R—B1 mate.* A third way is *1 . . . B—R5ch,* etc. Poor cooperation by White's pieces.

99. *1 Q—Q8ch, K—B2; 2 Kt—K5 mate.* Black's material advantage was worthless in view of his retarded development.

100. *1 B—Kt5ch, P—B3; 2 R—K7 mate.* The blocking motif makes an agreeable impression.

101. *1 . . . Kt—B6ch; 2 K—R1, Kt x P mate.* Or *2 K—B1, Kt(5)—Q7 mate!* Such a finish is rare indeed in the annals of master chess.

102. *1 . . . Q—Kt8ch; 2 R x Q, Kt—B7 mate.* The clearance theme continues to produce striking mates. Even *1 . . . Q x Rch* does the trick.

43

MATE IN TWO MOVES

DIAGRAM 103
White moves
Black: KUERSCHNER

White: TARRASCH
Nuremberg, 1893

DIAGRAM 104
Black moves
Black: HAMPTON

White: CHAROSH
Postal Game, 1943

DIAGRAM 105
White moves
Black: EISENSCHMIDT

White: CLEMENS
St. Petersburg, 1890

DIAGRAM 106
White moves
Black: AMATEUR

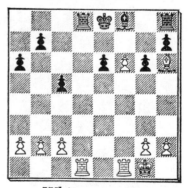

White: RATHER
Bangalore, 1944

DIAGRAM 107
White moves
Black: MACZUSKY

White: LINDEHN
Paris, 1863

DIAGRAM 108
White moves
Black: WEISS

White: SHIPLEY
Philadelphia, 1889

103. *1* Q—Kt6*ch*, P x Q; 2 B x P *mate*. The King is raked by the crossfire of the hostile Bishops.

104. *1* . . . Q x P*ch*; 2 K x Q, R—R4 *mate*. White's King didn't have a single friend left in the whole world.

105. *1* Q—B7*ch!*, Kt x Q; 2 Kt—K6 *mate*. A real problem mate.

106. *1* P—B7*ch*, K—K2; 2 B—Kt5 *mate*. Black suffers for having failed to castle.

107. *1* B—B6*ch*, Q x B [or *1* . . . Q—K2]; 2 Q x R *mate*. No development. It is not to be wondered at that such conclusions are rare in modern play.

108. *1* B—B5*ch*, K—Q3; 2 B—K7 *mate*. Perfect coordination against complete lack of it.

MATE IN TWO MOVES

DIAGRAM 109
Black moves
Black: TARRASCH

White: ALLIES
Nuremberg, 1904

DIAGRAM 110
White moves
Black: DUFF

White: VAN ESSEN
Long Beach, 1945

DIAGRAM 111
Black moves
Black: RANKEN

White: GRUNDY
London, 1893

DIAGRAM 112
Black moves
Black: TARRASCH

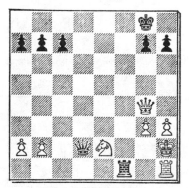

White: RIEMANN
Leipzig, 1893

DIAGRAM 113
White moves
Black: TCHIGORIN

White: STEINITZ
Match, 1892

DIAGRAM 114
White moves
Black: ROGERS

White: MRS. HOGG
Postal Game, 1945

109. 1 . . . R x R ch; 2 Q x R, Q x P mate. White's Queen was overworked.

110. 1 Q—K7ch, Kt x Q; 2 Kt—B6 mate. Reminiscent of 105.

111. 1 . . . Kt—Kt6ch; 2 RP x Kt [or *2 BP x Kt*], *Q—K8 mate.* Black "got thar fustest with the mostest men."

112. 1 . . . R—B7ch; 2 K—Kt1, Q—K8 mate. With a piece ahead, White was curiously helpless.

113. 1 Q x Kt ch, K—B4; 2 Q—B4 mate. Conclusion of a famous combination. White also had *2 P—Kt4 mate.*

114. 1 P—B7ch, R x P; 2 R—R8 mate. This was preceded by a Queen sacrifice.

MATE IN TWO MOVES

DIAGRAM 115
White moves
Black: AMATEUR

White: MACDONNELL
London, 1830

DIAGRAM 116
White moves
Black: BURN

White: MARSHALL
Ostend, 1905

DIAGRAM 117
White moves
Black: YUDKOVSKY

White: PANOV
Moscow, 1929

DIAGRAM 118
White moves
Black: KIESERITZKY

White: ANDERSSEN
London, 1851

DIAGRAM 119
White moves
Black: SCHELFHOUT

White: KMOCH
Amsterdam, 1934

DIAGRAM 120
White moves
Black: ROMBERG

White: TARRASCH
Nuremberg, 1893

115. 1 Kt—Kt5*ch*, K—Kt1; 2 Q x P *mate.* White's Bishop is malicious at long range.

116. 1 Q—B4*ch*, P—Kt4; 2 Q—B6 *mate.* Or 1 R x Kt*ch*, P x R; 2 Q—B6 *mate.* Black's deficit in development is appalling.

117. 1 R x P*ch*, Q—R2; 2 Q or R x Q *mate.* Easy!

118. 1 Q—B6*ch*, Kt x Q; 2 B—K7 *mate.* Black had a field day gobbling Rooks.

119. 1 R—B5*ch!*, B x R [if 1 . . . R—Kt4, White can choose from among three mating methods]; 2 Kt—B4 *mate.*

120. 1 B—Kt5*ch*, K—Kt3; 2 Kt(2)—B4 *mate.* Tarrasch sacrificed his Queen for this position. Giving the odds of Queen's Rook did not trouble him at all.

49

MATE IN TWO MOVES

DIAGRAM 121
White moves
Black: MIESES

White: DENKER
Hastings, 1945–46

DIAGRAM 122
White moves
Black: DURAS

White: SPIELMANN
Scheveningen, 1905

DIAGRAM 123
White moves
Black: AMATEUR

White: TEICHMANN

DIAGRAM 124
White moves
Black: ANDERSSEN

White: ZUKERTORT
Breslau, 1865

DIAGRAM 125
White moves
Black: WALTER

White: SPIELMANN
Trentschin-Teplitz, 1928

DIAGRAM 126
White moves
Black: VAN PRAAG

White: HEIJMANS
Amsterdam, 1851

SOLUTIONS

121. 1 R—K7*ch*, K—B1; 2 R x R *mate*. Another sad case of Pawn-grabbing.

122. 1 R x R*ch*, K x Kt; 2 Q—Kt5 *mate*. Black should have castled while he had the opportunity.

123. 1 Q x Kt*ch!*, R x Q; 2 B x P *mate*. The defending Knight had to be removed.

124. 1 Q—Kt5*ch* [more spectacular than 1 B—Kt5*ch*, which also does the trick], P x Q; 2 B x P *mate*. The end of a twelve-move game. How Anderssen must have blushed!

125. 1 Q x Kt*ch!*, B x Q; 2 Kt x P *mate*. "A bit of Morphy."

126. 1 R x P*ch*, K x R; 2 Q—R5 *mate*. Black failed to foresee this.

51

MATE IN TWO MOVES

DIAGRAM 127
White moves
Black: KOLB

White: TARRASCH
Nuremberg, 1893

DIAGRAM 128
White moves
Black: AMATEUR

White: ZUKERTORT
Berlin, 1869

DIAGRAM 129
Black moves
Black: BLAKE

White: MICHELL
London, 1920

DIAGRAM 130
White moves
Black: ST. LEON

White: KIESERITZKY
Paris, 1849

DIAGRAM 131
White moves
Black: HOWELL

White: PILLSBURY
New York, 1900

DIAGRAM 132
White moves
Black: McCUDDEN

White: SAMUELS
New York, 1925

127. 1 Q—B8*ch!*, R x Q; 2 Kt—Q7 *mate.* A charming smothered mate.

128. 1 R—Kt8*ch!*, R x R; 2 Kt—B7 *mate.* A similar specimen. Aside from being brilliant, the Rook check is the only way to win.

129. 1 . . . B—Kt7*ch;* 2 K —Kt1, Kt—B6 *mate.* The conclusion of a virulent attack.

130. 1 Q—Q8*ch,* K x Q; 2 R—B8 *mate.* Black's enormous material advantage is nullified by his lack of development.

131. 1 Q x Kt*ch,* Q x Q; 2 B—B7 *mate.* Pillsbury played blindfold.

132. 1 Kt—K4*ch* [or *1* Kt—Kt5*ch*], K—K2; 2 Q—B7 *mate.* An exposed King plus poor development.

MATE IN TWO MOVES

DIAGRAM 133
White moves
Black: AMATEUR

White: STEINITZ
London, 1863

DIAGRAM 134
White moves
Black: EUWE

White: MORRISON
London, 1922

DIAGRAM 135
White moves
Black: AMATEUR

White: ZUKERTORT
London, 1877

DIAGRAM 136
White moves
Black: AMATEUR

White: CANAL

DIAGRAM 137
Black moves
Black: STEINITZ

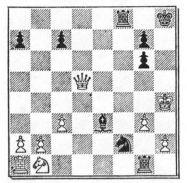

White: AMATEUR
London, 1864

DIAGRAM 138
White moves
Black: AMATEUR

White: ZUKERTORT
Berlin, 1869

133. *1* P x R*ch*, K x Kt [or *1* . . . K—B1; 2 B—R6 *mate* or *1* . . . K—Q1; 2 P—B7 *mate*]; *2* B—B4 *mate*. Steinitz sacrificed the Queen for this pretty position.

134. *1* Q x R*ch;* K x Q*;* 2 R—Kt8 *mate*. Incredible but true.

135. *1* Q x BP*ch,* P x Q [*1* . . . Q—B2 still allows mate next move]; 2 B—R6 *mate*.

136. *1* Q x P*ch!,* P x Q*;* 2 B—R6 *mate*. White parted with two Rooks to get this mate, which is basically the same as in the previous position.

137. *1* . . . R—B5*ch;* 2 P x R [or *2* P—Kt4, R x P *mate*], R—Kt5 *mate*. Steinitz's sacrifice of the Queen at an earlier stage was based on White's faulty development.

138. *1* R—Q6*ch,* R x R*;* 2 Kt—K6 *mate*. A nasty double check.

55

MATE IN TWO MOVES

DIAGRAM 139
White moves
Black: WINTER

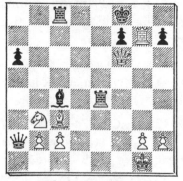

White: MARGOLIS
Chicago, 1946

DIAGRAM 140
Black moves
Black: MORPHY

White: SCHULTEN
New York, 1857

DIAGRAM 141
Black moves
Black: MOTTA

White: PEREIRA
Brazil, 1937

DIAGRAM 142
Black moves
Black: YANKOVICH

White: MANKO
Postal Game, 1900

56

DIAGRAM 143
White moves
Black: JAFFE

White: ALLIES
Havre, 1912

DIAGRAM 144
White moves
Black: DELMAR

White: TEED
New York, 1896

139. *1* R—Kt8*ch*, K x R; *2* Q—Kt7 *mate.* Look at Black's Queen. *2* Q—R8 *mate* is another way.

140. *1* . . . Kt—B4*ch* [another way is *1* . . . Q—B7*ch*; *2* K—Kt5, P—B3 *mate* or *2* . . . Q—Kt6 *mate*]; *2* K—Kt5, Q—R4 *mate.* Was White's trip with the King necessary?

141. *1* . . . Q—Kt6; *2* P x Kt, Q—R5 *mate.* White threw away the advantage of the first move.

142. *1* . . . Q x R*ch*; *2* B x Q, Kt—B6 *mate.* From one of the shortest games on record.

143. *1* Kt—B6*ch*, K—B1; *2* Q—K8 *mate.* The allies were too much for the master.

144. *1* Q x P*ch*, R x Q; *2* B—Kt6 *mate.* Black was a player of master strength!

57

MATE IN TWO MOVES

DIAGRAM 145
White moves
Black: AMATEUR

White: STEINITZ
London, 1862

DIAGRAM 146
White moves
Black: NILSSON

White: KROGIUS
Helsinki, 1946

DIAGRAM 147
White moves
Black: ENDZELIUS

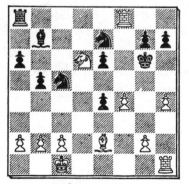

White: PLECI
Buenos Aires, 1939

DIAGRAM 148
White moves
Black: DRUVA

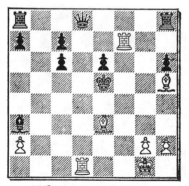

White: NIMZOVICH
Riga, 1919

DIAGRAM 149
White moves
Black: KUJOTH

White: FRIEDMAN
U. S. Junior Championship, 1946

DIAGRAM 150
White moves
Black: PILHAL

White: STEINITZ
Vienna, 1862

145. 1 P—Q7*ch*, Q x P [or *1* . . . B x P]; 2 Q—B8 *mate.* Black's neglected development is typical of the period.

146. 1 Q x P*ch*, K x Q; 2 R—R5 *mate.* A familiar but always attractive theme.

147. 1 P—R5*ch*, K—R3; 2 Kt—B7 *mate.* Conclusion of a remarkable combinative game.

148. 1 B—B4*ch*, K—K5; 2 B—B3 *mate.* From a game in which Nimzovich gave Queen odds!

149. 1 R—Kt7*ch!*, K x R; 2 Q—R7 *mate.* Another neat example of the clearance sacrifice.

150. 1 Kt—B6*ch*, K—B1 [or *1* . . . K—Q1]; 2 B x Kt *mate.* A Queen sacrifice was the prelude to this one.

MATE IN TWO MOVES

DIAGRAM 151
White moves
Black: THOMAS

White: LASKER
London, 1912

DIAGRAM 152
White moves
Black: NEWMAN

White: BOWLEY
London, 1945

DIAGRAM 153
Black moves
Black: KONSTANTINOPOLSKY

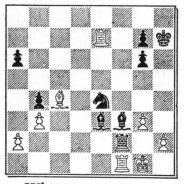

White: ZAGORYANSKY
Sverdlovsk, 1943

DIAGRAM 154
White moves
Black: ELISKASES

White: LILIENTHAL
Ujpest, 1934

DIAGRAM 155
Black moves
Black: ATKINS

White: TARTAKOVER
London, 1922

DIAGRAM 156
Black moves
Black: CZERNIAK

White: FOGEL
Jerusalem, 1935

151. 1 R—R2*ch*, K—Kt8; 2 K—Q2 *mate* or 2 O—O—O *mate!* Another way is *1* O—O—O, when Black is helpless against 2 QR—Kt1 or 2 R—R2 *mate*.

152. 1 R—Kt8*ch*, Kt x R; 2 Q—Kt7 *mate*. Black castled into disaster.

153. 1 . . . R—Kt7*ch*; 2 K —R1, R—Kt8 *mate*. In both cases Black must find the right discovered check.

154. 1 Q—Kt6*ch*, K—B1 [or *1* . . . K—R1; 2 Q—Kt7 *mate*]; 2 B—B5 *mate*. Black was threatening *1* . . . R x P*ch*, etc.

155. *1* . . . Q—B4*ch*; 2 K—Kt3, Q—B7 *mate*. The end of a King hunt, starting from White's QB1.

156. *1* . . . Q x Kt*ch*; 2 K x Q, R—B8 *mate*. White's retarded development left the first rank unguarded.

MATE IN TWO MOVES

DIAGRAM 157
Black moves
Black: RATHER

White: McCORMICK
New York, 1946

DIAGRAM 158
Black moves
Black: ALBIN

White: BAIRD
New York, 1894

DIAGRAM 159
White moves
Black: AMATEUR

White: BJERKNESS
Christiania, 1915

DIAGRAM 160
White moves
Black: AMATEUR

White: HOROWITZ
Austin, 1941

DIAGRAM 161
White moves
Black: BURN

White: OWEN
London, 1887

DIAGRAM 162
White moves
Black: GOSLIN

White: VANDERVOORT
Postal Game, 1922

157. 1 . . . R x P*ch; 2* B x R [or *2* K—R1, Q x P *mate*], Q x B *mate*. The King's Knight file is too much for White.

158. 1 . . . R—Kt8*ch; 2* Kt x R, Q—Kt7 *mate*. Such clearance sacrifices are always pleasing.

159. 1 Kt x P*ch*, Kt x Kt; *2* Kt—Kt6 *mate*. This is so sudden!

160. 1 B x P*ch*, K x B [or *1* . . . K—B2; *2* Q—Kt7 *mate*]; *2* Q—Kt7 *mate*. Black's King shivers in the icy blast.

161. 1 Q x P*ch*, Kt x Q [or *1* . . . Kt—Kt2; *2* Q x Kt *mate*]; *2* B x Kt *mate*. Black castled into it.

162. 1 R—R6*ch*, P x R; *2* Q—Kt4 *mate*. A neat self-blocking motif. Less artistic but equally effective is *1* Q—B5*ch*, K—R5 [if *1* . . . P—Kt4; *2* Q—R3 *mate*]; *2* P—Kt3 *mate* or *2* R—Q4 *mate*.

MATE IN TWO MOVES

DIAGRAM 163
White moves
Black: ENGLUND

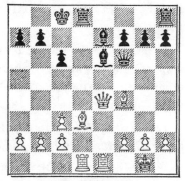

White: LASKER
Scheveningen, 1913

DIAGRAM 164
White moves
Black: BALOGH

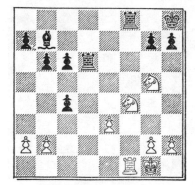

White: A. STEINER
Pistyan, 1922

DIAGRAM 165
Black moves
Black: PILLSBURY

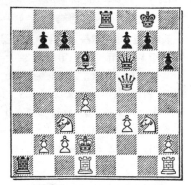

White: McCONNELL
New Orleans, 1899

DIAGRAM 166
White moves
Black: COUVEE

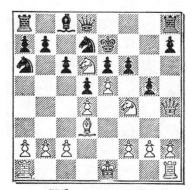

White: SPEYER
Amsterdam, 1902

DIAGRAM 167
Black moves
Black: MARCHAND

White: HARTINGSVELT
Scheveningen, 1915

DIAGRAM 168
Black moves
Black: RATHER

White: WEINSTOCK
New York, 1946

163. *1* Q x P*ch*, P x Q; *2* B—R6 *mate*. This has become a familiar but always pleasing theme.

164. *1* Kt—Kt6*ch*, P x Kt [*1* . . . R x Kt is no better]; *2* R x R *mate*. White prepared this with a clever sacrifice of the exchange.

165. *1* . . . Q x P*ch*; *2* Q—Q3, B—B5 *mate*. Another case of risky Queen-side castling.

166. *1* Q x P*ch*, R x Q [if *1* . . . K—B1; *2* Q—B7 or Kt —Kt6 or Kt x P *mate*]; *2* Kt—Kt6 *mate*. A drastic and amusing punishment for Black's feeble opening play.

167. *1* . . . Kt—Q6; *2* P—R7, Kt—B7 *mate*. The same finish would have been possible with White's Pawn advanced one rank!

168. *1* . . . R x P*ch*; *2* P x R, Q x P *mate*.

MATE IN TWO MOVES

DIAGRAM 169
White moves
Black: KOTOV

White: O. BERNSTEIN
Groningen, 1946

DIAGRAM 170
White moves
Black: AMATEUR

White: NIMZOVICH
Riga, 1899

DIAGRAM 171
Black moves
Black: STAHLBERG

White: SCHROEDER
Santiago, 1946

DIAGRAM 172
White moves
Black: BURN

White: MARSHALL
Paris, 1900

DIAGRAM 173
White moves
Black: JACOBSEN

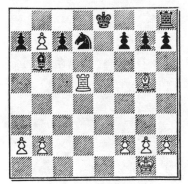

White: GIERSING
Copenhagen, 1917

DIAGRAM 174
Black moves
Black: NIMZOVICH

White: FAHRNI
Carlsbad, 1911

169. 1 Q x P*ch!*, P x Q; *2* R(QR8)—Kt8 *mate.* Truth is stranger than fiction.

170. 1 Q—B5*ch*, Kt x Q; *2* P—K6 *mate.* This pretty combination was played by the father of the famous master.

171. 1 . . . Q x P; *2* P x Q [other moves allow *2* . . . Q—R8 *mate*], Kt—R6 *mate.*

172. 1 R—R8*ch*, K x R; *2* Q—R7 *mate.* A "quickie."

173. 1 P—Kt8(Q)*ch*, Kt x Q; *2* R—Q8 *mate.* Promotion to Rook also accomplishes the mate.

174. 1 . . . R—K8*ch*; *2* R x R [or *2* Q x R, Q—Kt7 *mate*], Q—R8 *mate.* Note how the Rook immolates himself to clear the Bishop's diagonal.

MATE IN TWO MOVES

DIAGRAM 175
Black moves
Black: DONOVAN

White: ULVESTAD
Ventnor City, 1940

DIAGRAM 176
White moves
Black: GIBAUD

White: LAZARD
Paris, 1910

DIAGRAM 177
White moves
Black: REESE

White: ARMITAGE
London, 1946

DIAGRAM 178
White moves
Black: LEONHARDT

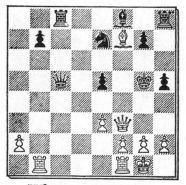

White: SCHLECHTER
Carlsbad, 1911

SOLUTIONS

DIAGRAM 179
White moves
Black: KOSTICH

White: BARRY
Boston, 1917

DIAGRAM 180
White moves
Black: KURSCHNER

White: HROMADKA
Hamburg, 1910

175. *1 . . .* Kt—Kt5*ch;* 2 K—R3, Kt—B5 *mate.* Artistic play.

176. *1* R—K8*ch,* Kt x R; 2 Q—B8 *mate.* Concluding one of the most brilliant games on record.

177. *1* Q x P*ch,* K x Q; 2 R—R4 *mate.*

178. *1* P—R4*ch,* K x P [or *1 . . .* K—R3; 2 Q x P *mate*]; 2 Q—Kt3 *mate.* Black's opening play left much to be desired.

179. *1* Q—Kt6*ch,* Kt x Q; 2 P x Kt *mate.* The division of the Black forces proved disastrous.

180. *1* Kt—B5*ch,* K—R4; 2 Q—R4 *mate.* Here again a hard-pressed King gets no help from his fair-weather friends. 2 P—Kt4 *mate* is an alternative method.

MATE IN TWO MOVES

DIAGRAM 181
White moves
Black: DUFRESNE

White: NEUMANN
Berlin, 1863

DIAGRAM 182
White moves
Black: FIEDLER

White: TARRASCH
Nuremberg, 1892

DIAGRAM 183
White moves
Black: DAVIDOV

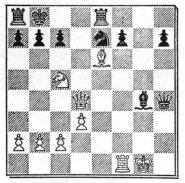

White: TCHIGORIN
St. Petersburg, 1891

DIAGRAM 184
Black moves
Black: PHILIDOR

White: LEICESTER
London, 1788

DIAGRAM 185
White moves
Black: LEE

White: JANOWSKI
London, 1899

DIAGRAM 186
White moves
Black: OTTO

White: TCHIGORIN
St. Petersburg, 1893

181. 1 Q x P*ch,* P x Q; 2 B x R *mate.* The opening of the King Bishop's diagonal permits a fine finish.

182. 1 Q—Kt4*ch,* B x Q; 2 B—B7 *mate.* Tarrasch gives Rook odds and mates in 16 moves!

183. 1 Kt—R6*ch,* P x Kt; 2 Q—Kt4 *mate.* From one of the finest Muzios on record.

184. 1 . . . Kt—Q6*ch;* 2 K—B1, Q—Q8 *mate.* White's King is neatly fenced in.

185. 1 B—K8*ch,* K x B; 2 Q—B7 *mate.* Very pretty play. Janowski would not part with a Bishop for anything short of mate!

186. 1 R x B*ch,* K—R1; 2 R x P *mate* [or 2 R—Kt8 *mate*]. This was the game finish; but a more elegant course is 1 R x R*ch,* K x R; 2 Q—B7 *mate.*

MATE IN TWO MOVES

DIAGRAM 187
Black moves
Black: COLLIJN

White: HALLGARTEN
Ostend, 1906

DIAGRAM 188
White moves
Black: HODGES

White: STEINITZ
New York, 1891

DIAGRAM 189
Black moves
Black: BODEN

White: MACDONNELL
London, 1860

DIAGRAM 190
Black moves
Black: LEVENFISH

White: RABINOVICH
Moscow, 1927

72

DIAGRAM 191
Black moves
Black: HIRSCHFELD

White: MAYET
London, 1861

DIAGRAM 192
White moves
Black: STEINITZ

White: FAEHNDRICH
Vienna, 1897

187. *1* . . . R x P*ch;* 2 P x R, Q—R7 *mate.* What could be simpler?

188. *1* Q x P*ch,* R x Q; 2 R—Kt8 *mate.* Steinitz played "blindfold."

189. *1* . . . Kt x P*ch* [or *1* . . . R—Kt3*ch;* 2 Q x R, R—Q8 *mate*]; 2 R x Kt, R—K8 *mate.* The pretty sequel to one of the finest Queen sacrifices ever made. Black can also begin with *1* . . . R—Q8*ch.*

190. *1* . . . Kt—R5*ch;* 2 K—K1 [if 2 K—Kt1, Q—Kt5 *mate*], Kt x Kt *mate.* This game is one of the shortest ever played between masters.

191. *1* . . . Q—Kt6*ch* [the Queen can also check at Kt4 or Kt5, so that if 2 K—B2, Q—Kt6 *mate*]; 2 K—R1, Q—Kt7 *mate.*

192. *1* Kt x P*ch,* K—Q2; 2 B—Kt5 *mate.* White had sacrificed a Rook in preparation for this finish.

73

Mate in Three Moves

MOVES BY the Queen are the key to most of the problems in our final section; and this is as it should be, for the Queen, being the most powerful piece, is the soul of the attack.

And it is the attack which forms the subject matter of this book. In the final section, which you are about to begin, the examples may be said to be truly complicated. They are now a real challenge. The conceptions in many cases are rather subtle; there are misleading alternatives which are not quite good enough; there are also alternatives which compete successfully for the honor of forcing checkmate in three moves.

As you work on these problems, you will acquire a bit of information which is basic but often unrealized by the chessplayer: *the attack is the means whereby we seek to enforce our will on our opponent.* If the attack is successful, we achieve our objective (in this case checkmate). When you complete this section, you will know why the attack is important, you will know why attacking skill must be cultivated. *Challenge to Chessplayers* was written to drive these points home.

MATE IN THREE MOVES

DIAGRAM 193
White moves
Black: GORER

White: GARCIA VERA
Rosario, 1939

DIAGRAM 194
Black moves
Black: HORWITZ

White: SCHULTEN
London, 1846

DIAGRAM 195
White moves
Black: AMATEUR

White: DUS-CHOTIMIRSKY
Hamburg, 1910

DIAGRAM 196
White moves
Black: AMATEUR

White: LEWIS
London, 1840

DIAGRAM 197
White moves
Black: SKLAROFF

White: DRASIN
Philadelphia, 1935

DIAGRAM 198
White moves
Black: SZEN

White: HARRWITZ
London, 1851

193. *1* Kt x P*ch*, B x Kt; *2* Q x Q*ch*, P x Q; *3* B—R6 *mate*.

194. *1* . . . Q—B8*ch*; *2* K x Q, B—Q6*ch*; *3* K—K1, R—B8 *mate*. Several generations have relished this one.

195. *1* R x B*ch*, P x R [if *1* . . . Q—B2; *2* Q x Q *mate*]; *2* Q x P*ch* [more elegant but not faster than *2* B x P*ch*], R x Q; *3* B x P *mate*. Essentially this is the same mate as in Example 193.

196. *1* R—K8*ch*, B—B1; *2* B—R6, any; *3* R x B *mate*. Economical utilization of White's development.

197. *1* Kt—K8*ch*, K—K4; *2* Q—Kt3*ch* [or *2* Q—Kt7*ch* or *2* Q—R8*ch*, K—K5; *3* Q—Q4 *mate*], K—K5; *3* Kt—B6 *mate* [or *3* Q—B4 *mate* or *3* R—Q4 *mate*]. Both the setting and the finish are unconventional.

198. *1* R—K8!, Q x R [*2* Q—Kt7 *mate* was threatened]; *2* Q—B6*ch*, R—Kt2; *3* Q x R *mate*. White's first move deflected Black's Queen from the defense.

MATE IN THREE MOVES

DIAGRAM 199
White moves
Black: AMATEUR

White: MORPHY
New York, 1857

DIAGRAM 200
White moves
Black: ASZTALOS

White: LOVAS
Budapest, 1915

DIAGRAM 201
Black moves
Black: STEINITZ

White: ROSENTHAL
London, 1883

DIAGRAM 202
Black moves
Black: JANOWSKI

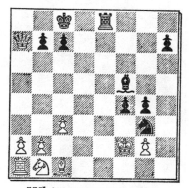

White: TAUBENHAUS
Paris, 1905

78

DIAGRAM 203
White moves
Black: HANHAM

White: BLACKBURNE
New York, 1889

DIAGRAM 204
White moves
Black: LICHTNER

White: ERDOS
Vienna, 1923

199. *1* R—B8*ch*, Q x R; *2* R x Q*ch*, R x R; *3* Q x P *mate.* The original "épaulette mate." On the Black King it looks good.

200. *1* B—Kt8*ch*, B—B2 [if *1* . . . K—Q2; *2* Q—B5 *mate*]; *2* B x B*ch*, K—Q2; *3* Q—B5 *mate.* On the 13th move, White had a forced mate in seven!

201. *1* . . . P—B7*ch*; *2* K x P [if *2* Q x P, Q—R8 *mate*], Q—Kt7*ch*; *3* K—K3, Q—B6 *mate.* The end of a brilliancy prize combination.

202. *1* . . . R—K7*ch*; *2* K—Kt1, R—K8*ch*; *3* K—B2, R—B8 *mate.* White's Queen is an interested spectator.

203. *1* R—R3*ch*, K—Kt2; *2* B—R6*ch*, K moves; *3* B x R *mate.* See above.

204. *1* Q—Kt6, Q—Kt1 [if *1* . . . P x Kt; *2* Q—R7 *mate* and if *1* . . . Kt x Q; *2* Kt—B7 *mate*]; *2* Q—R7*ch*, Q x Q; *3* Kt—B7 *mate.* Delightful! Or *2* Kt—B7*ch*, Q x Kt; *3* Q—R7 *mate.*

MATE IN THREE MOVES

DIAGRAM 205
White moves
Black: AMATEUR

White: NAPIER
1904

DIAGRAM 206
White moves
Black: STEPHENS

White: S. BERNSTEIN
Ventnor City, 1940

DIAGRAM 207
White moves
Black: KMOCH

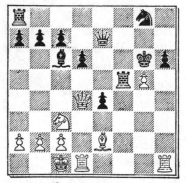

White: WEENINK
London, 1927

DIAGRAM 208
White moves
Black: BAER

White: BLASS
Postal Game, 1933

DIAGRAM 209
White moves
Black: GRUENFELD

White: SPIELMANN
Carlsbad, 1929

DIAGRAM 210
Black moves
Black: LIBAIRE

White: FOX
New York, 1906

205. *1* Q—Kt6*ch*, B x Q; *2* Kt—Kt5*ch!*, P x Kt; *3* P x B *mate.* The Allgaier always produces brilliant chess.

206. *1* B—B7*ch*, R x B; *2* Q—Kt6*ch*, K—B1 [or *2* . . . R—Kt2; *3* Q x R *mate*]; *3* Q x R *mate.* Just punishment for Black's miserable play.

207. *1* B—R5*ch*, K x P [or *1* . . . K—R2; *2* P—Kt6 *mate!*]; *2* QR—Kt1*ch*, K—B5; *3* Kt—K2 *mate.* No place for a King.

208. *1* R(3)—R3!, B x R [if *1* . . . B x Q; *2* R—R8 mate]; *2* Q—R7*ch*, K—B1; *3* Q—R8 *mate.*

209. *1* P—R6*ch*, K—R1 [*1* . . . K—Kt1 allows the same finish]; *2* Q—B6*ch*, K—Kt1; *3* Q—Kt7 *mate.* Black had failed to take preventive measures against the break-up of his King-side.

210. *1* . . . B—Q5*ch*; *2* K—Kt2 [if *2* Kt x B, Q—B7 *mate*], Q—K5*ch*; *3* K—Kt3, B—B7 or . . . Q—B6 *mate.* The windup of a very brilliant attack.

81

MATE IN THREE MOVES

DIAGRAM 211
White moves
Black: PALMER

White: YATES
Glasgow, 1911

DIAGRAM 212
White moves
Black: DREWITT

White: WINTER
London, 1929

DIAGRAM 213
White moves
Black: SEITZ

White: PRZEPIORKA
Hastings, 1925–26

DIAGRAM 214
White moves
Black: GOSSIP

White: SCHALLOPP
Manchester, 1890

DIAGRAM 215
White moves
Black: AMATEUR

White: CAPABLANCA
Moscow, 1914

DIAGRAM 216
Black moves
Black: RETI

White: AMATEUR
Vienna, 1918

211. *1* Q—K7*ch*, K—Kt3; 2 Q x QP*ch*, K—Kt4; 3 Q—B6 *mate*. Satisfying conclusion to an implacable King hunt.

212. *1* Q—R5*ch*, K—Kt2 [if *1* . . . K x Q; 2 R—R3 *mate*]; 2 Q—R7*ch*, K moves; 3 Q—B7 *mate*.

213. *1* R x Kt*ch*, R x R [if *1* . . . K—K2; 2 Q—K6 *mate*]; 2 Q—K6*ch*, K—B1; 3 Kt—Q7 *mate*. The King was pummelled by White's pieces.

214. *1* Q x RP*ch*, K—Kt1; 2 Q—Kt5*ch*, K moves; 3 R—R6 *mate*. The isolation of Black's King is a serious reflection on his previous play.

215. *1* R—K1*ch*, K x P; 2 P—B3*ch*, K—Q6; 3 R—Q5 *mate*. A highly imaginative finish.

216. *1* . . . R x B*ch*; 2 K x R, Q—Kt6*ch*; 3 K—R1, Q—R6 *mate*. Black's previous sacrifices paid off because White's pieces were useless.

83

MATE IN THREE MOVES

DIAGRAM 217
Black moves
Black: TCHIGORIN

White: ARNOLD
St. Petersburg, 1885

DIAGRAM 218
Black moves
Black: RICHMAN

White: GRESSER
New York, 1945

DIAGRAM 219
Black moves
Black: MAROCZY

White: HAVASI
Budapest, 1892

DIAGRAM 220
White moves
Black: MEIZER

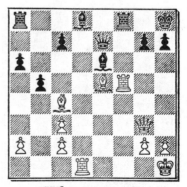

White: MARCO
Czernowitz, 1900

DIAGRAM 221
Black moves
Black: BLACKBURNE

White: GAMMAN
London, 1869

DIAGRAM 222
White moves
Black: PARNELL

White: MACKENZIE
New York, 1890

SOLUTIONS

217. *1* . . . Q x P*ch!;* 2 K x Q, B—B6*ch;* 3 K—B1 [if 3 K—Kt3, B—B7 *mate*], Kt—R7 *mate*. Tchigorin played this game blindfold.

218. *1* . . . Q x P*ch;* 2 K x Q, P x Kt*ch;* 3 K—Kt2, R—R7 *mate*. The break-up of White's King-side Pawns had unfortunate consequences.

219. *1* . . . Kt—B4*ch;* 2 K—Q2, R—Q8*ch;* 3 K—B2, Kt—K6 *mate*. Beautiful cooperation by the Black pieces!

220. 1 Q x P*ch*, Q x Q; 2 R x R*ch*, B—Kt1; 3 R x B *mate*. White's Bishops were too strong.

221. *1* . . . Kt(5) x B*ch;* 2 P x Kt, R x P*ch;* 3 K x R, Q—R2 *mate*.

222. 1 Q x Kt*ch*, K x Q; 2 Kt—B3*ch*, K—B4; 3 R—B1 *mate*. The Allgaier has been a fertile source of brilliancies. *1* Kt—B3 mates less flamboyantly.

MATE IN THREE MOVES

DIAGRAM 223
Black moves
Black: TCHIGORIN

White: AMATEUR
St. Petersburg, 1875

DIAGRAM 224
Black moves
Black: MAROCZY

White: ZAMBELLY
Postal Game, 1897–98

DIAGRAM 225
White moves
Black: FAURE

White: D'AUMILLER
Verona, 1893

DIAGRAM 226
Black moves
Black: THOMAS

White: EUWE
Hastings, 1945–46

SOLUTIONS

DIAGRAM 227
Black moves
Black: PETROFF

White: HOFFMANN
Warsaw, 1844

DIAGRAM 228
White moves
Black: MUMELTER

White: AMATEUR
Vienna, 1896

223. *1 . . .* R x B*ch;* 2 P x R, Q—R8*ch!;* 3 Kt x Q, R—Kt7 *mate.* A characteristically elegant mate by the great Russian master.

224. *1 . . .* P—R3*ch;* 2 K—B4, P—Kt4*ch;* 3 K—K5, Q—K3 *mate.* The conclusion of a magnificent combination.

225. *1* P—Q4! [threatens 2 P—B4 *mate*], B x P; 2 Kt—B6*ch,* K—R3; 3 R x B *mate.* Sequel to a Queen sacrifice.

226. *1 . . .* Kt—Kt8*ch;* 2 K x P, R—R2*ch;* 3 Q—R6, R(2) x Q *mate.*

227. *1 . . .* R—B4*ch;* 2 K—Kt4, P—R4*ch;* 3 K—R3, R—B6 *mate.* Conclusion of one of the classics from the so-called Golden Age of chess.

228. *1* Q x P*ch,* K x Q; 2 R—R7*ch,* K—B1; 3 R—B7 *mate.* White sacrificed a Rook to get this position.

87

MATE IN THREE MOVES

DIAGRAM 229
White moves
Black: SCHWARZ

White: BLACKBURNE

Vienna, 1873

DIAGRAM 230
Black moves
Black: ATKINS

White: TRESLING

Amsterdam, 1899

DIAGRAM 231
Black moves
Black: FISHER

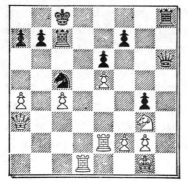

White: BAIN

Stockholm, 1937

DIAGRAM 232
White moves
Black: BURN

White: BLACKBURNE

Hastings, 1895

DIAGRAM 233
White moves
Black: MRAZEK

White: SEIDMANN
Bratislava, 1936

DIAGRAM 234
Black moves
Black: STEINITZ

White: HAMPPE
Vienna, 1859

229. *1* R—K7*ch*, K—B1; *2* R—K8*ch*, K x R; *3* Q—K7 *mate*. White has put the pin to good use.

230. *1* . . . Q—R6*ch!*; *2* K x Q, Kt—K6*ch*; *3* K—R2, R—R1 *mate*. Out of a clear sky.

231. *1* . . . Q—R7*ch*; *2* K—B1, Q—R8*ch*; *3* Kt x Q, R x Kt *mate*. The Rook at K2 blocked the King's exit.

232. *1* Q—Q3*ch*, K—B4; *2* Q—Q4*ch*, K—Kt4; *3* Q—Kt4 *mate*. Blackburne had sacrificed a piece for this imaginative finish.

233. *1* Q x P*ch!*, K x Q; *2* R(1)—R7*ch*, K—K1; *3* B x P *mate*. Black had it coming to him: poor development.

234. *1* . . . Q—Q7*ch*; *2* K—Kt1, Q—Q8*ch*; *3* R x Q, R x R *mate*. An early Steinitz brilliancy.

MATE IN THREE MOVES

DIAGRAM 235
White moves
Black: GUDJU

White: ADDICKS

Prague, 1931

DIAGRAM 236
White moves
Black: PHILP

White: BLACKBURNE

London, 1875

DIAGRAM 237
White moves
Black: V. SCHEVE

White: TARRASCH

Breslau, 1880

DIAGRAM 238
Black moves
Black: DERRICKSON

White: AMATEUR

Philadelphia, 1860

DIAGRAM 239
White moves
Black: MORTIMER

White: POLLOCK
London, 1887

DIAGRAM 240
Black moves
Black: WARD

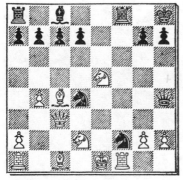

White: ROWE
London, 1876

235. *1* B x P*ch*, K x B; *2* Kt—Kt5*ch*, K—Kt1 [or *2 . . .* K—B3]; *3* Q—K6 *mate*. The proper outcome of Black's wretched development.

236. *1* Q—B5*ch* [or *1* Q—K4*ch*], K—Kt1; *2* Q—Kt6*ch*, B—Kt2; *3* Q x B *mate*. Black's material advantage was of no value.

237. *1* Q x Kt*ch*, R x Q; *2* R—B8*ch*, R—Q1; *3* B—Kt5 *mate*. The outcome of Black's Pawn-grabbing.

238. *1 . . .* Kt—Q5*ch!*; *2* K x R, Kt—K6*ch*; *3* K—B1, Kt —K7 *mate*. The prettiest way to win.

239. *1* Q x P*ch*, K x Q; *2* R—R4*ch*, Q—R3; *3* R x Q *mate*. A familiar motif.

240. *1 . . .* Kt—Q6*ch*; *2* K—Q1, Q—K8*ch*; *3* R x Q, Kt —B7 *mate*. A curious smothered mate.

MATE IN THREE MOVES

DIAGRAM 241
White moves
Black: ARNOLD

White: MARRIOTT
Postal Game, 1944

DIAGRAM 242
White moves
Black: CARO

White: SHOWALTER
Vienna, 1898

DIAGRAM 243
Black moves
Black: MARTINEZ

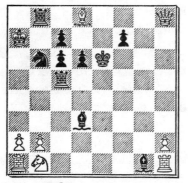

White: SHIPLEY
Philadelphia, 1889

92

DIAGRAM 244
White moves
Black: SATZINGER

White: TARRASCH
Munich, 1915

DIAGRAM 245
White moves
Black: GRINBERG

White: ALONI
Palestine Championship, 1945

DIAGRAM 246
White moves
Black: MACMURRAY

White: DENKER
New York, 1933

241. 1 Q—R6*ch*, Kt x Q; 2 B x Kt*ch*, K—Kt1; 3 P—B7 *mate*. A neat resource.

242. 1 Q—Kt8*ch* [the mating process can also begin with 1 R—K8*ch*], K x Q; 2 R—K8*ch*, R x R; 3 R x R *mate*.

243. 1 . . . R—R1*ch*; 2 K—Kt7, B—R3*ch*; 3 K x P, Kt—Q4 *mate*. Black sacrificed his Queen in order to drive White's King into the great open spaces.

244. 1 Kt—B7*ch*, K—Kt1; 2 R—R8*ch!*, Kt x R; 3 Kt—R6 *mate*. Beautiful sequel to a Queen sacrifice.

245. 1 Q—B5*ch*, K—Kt1; 2 Q—Kt6*ch*, K—B1; 3 B—Q6 *mate*.

246. 1 Kt—B7*ch*, K—B1; 2 R—Q8*ch*, Kt x R; 3 Q—K8 *mate*. Another way was 1 R—Q8*ch*, Kt x R; 2 Kt—Q6*ch* [or 2 Kt—B7*ch*], K—B1; 3 Q—K8 *mate*.

MATE IN THREE MOVES

DIAGRAM 247
Black moves
Black: TARRASCH

White: ECKART
Nuremberg, 1887

DIAGRAM 248
White moves
Black: WHITCOMB

White: HOROWITZ
Newburyport, 1946

DIAGRAM 249
White moves
Black: ALLIES

White: ZUKERTORT
Berlin, 1869

DIAGRAM 250
Black moves
Black: MIESES

White: CHRISTOFFEL
Hastings, 1945–46

DIAGRAM 251

White moves

Black: JENKINS

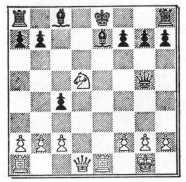

White: BRUNNEMER

New York, 1919

DIAGRAM 252

White moves

Black: SCHROEDER

White: TARRASCH

Nuremberg, 1894

247. *1 . . .* Q—B7*ch!;* 2 K x Q, R—Q8*ch;* 3 B—K3, B x B *mate.* White must have been under the impression that *he* had the attack!

248. *1* Kt—B6*ch,* P x Kt; 2 Q—Kt3*ch,* B—Kt5; 3 Q x B *mate.* Effective exploitation of the congested position of Black's King.

249. *1* Q x P*ch,* P x Q; 2 R x P*ch,* R—R2; 3 B x P *mate.* Conclusion of one of Zukertort's blindfold games.

250. *1 . . .* Q x RP*ch;* 2 K x Kt, R x B*ch;* 3 P x R [or 3 K x P, Q—R3 *mate*], Q—R5 *mate.* An astonishing combination for a man well over eighty.

251. *1* Kt—B7*ch,* K—B1; 2 Q—Q8*ch,* B x Q; 3 R—K8 *mate.* Such combinations must always be watched for when the King is stranded in the center.

252. *1* Q x P*ch,* K x Q; *2* P x P*ch,* K x P; *3* R—R6 *mate.*

MATE IN THREE MOVES

DIAGRAM 253
White moves
Black: BAKER

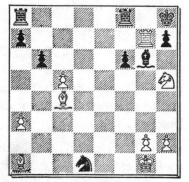

White: DENKER
New York, 1937

DIAGRAM 254
White moves
Black: STEINITZ

White: GRIMSHAW
London, 1878

DIAGRAM 255
White moves
Black: NORMAN

White: KAPSENBURG
Hastings, 1945–46

DIAGRAM 256
White moves
Black: MARSHALL

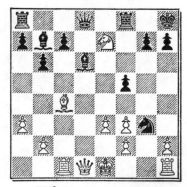

White: JOHNSTON
Match, 1900

DIAGRAM 257
Black moves
Black: S. BERNSTEIN

White: DONOVAN
Ventnor City, 1942

DIAGRAM 258
White moves
Black: TARTAKOVER

White: SPIELMANN
Munich, 1909

253. *1* R—Kt8*ch!*, R x R; 2 B x P*ch*, R—Kt2; *3* B x R *mate*. A remarkable finish with the Queens off the board.

254. *1* Q—Q6*ch*, KKt—K2; 2 Q—Q8*ch*, Kt x Q; *3* R x Kt *mate*. Probably the worst beating ever administered to Steinitz.

255. *1* Q x P*ch* [the mate can also begin with *1* P x P*ch* etc.], P x Q; 2 P—Kt6*ch*, P x P; *3* P x P *mate*. Drastic exploitation of Black's congested position.

256. *1* Kt—Kt6*ch*, P x Kt; 2 P x Kt*ch*, Q—R5; *3* R x Q *mate*. An imaginative finish.

257. *1* . . . Q x P*ch*; 2 K x Q, R—R3*ch*; *3* K—Kt3, R—R6 *mate*. Compare 218.

258. *1* Kt—K7*ch*, Kt x Kt; 2 B x P*ch*, Q x B; *3* Q x Q *mate*. Hardly surprising, in view of the inefficient placement of Black's pieces.

97

MATE IN THREE MOVES

DIAGRAM 259
White moves
Black: SCHROEDER

White: TARRASCH
Nuremberg, 1889

DIAGRAM 260
White moves
Black: WADE

White: GYLES
Wellington, 1945

DIAGRAM 261
Black moves
Black: POLLOCK

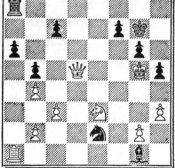
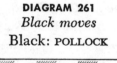

White: WEISS
New York, 1889

DIAGRAM 262
Black moves
Black: YATES

White: ALEKHINE
Carlsbad, 1923

DIAGRAM 263

Black moves

Black: JAENISCH

White: SCHUMOV

St. Petersburg, 1854

DIAGRAM 264

White moves

Black: RHYNDER

White: KUSSMAN

Geneva, 1936

259. *1* R—Q8*ch,* K—B2; *2* B—B4*ch,* B—K3 [or *2 . . .* Q—K3]; *3* Kt x P *mate.* Tarrasch gave Queen odds in this game!

260. *1* Kt—Kt6*ch,* K x B; *2* Kt x R*ch,* K—Kt1; *3* Q—R7 *mate.* The Black pieces were headed in the wrong direction.

261. *1 . . .* P—B3*ch;* 2 K —R4, B—B7*ch;* 3 P—Kt3, B x P *mate.* Conclusion of a charming combination which began with the Queen sacrifice.

262. *1 . . .* B—Kt8*ch;* 2 K —Kt3, Q—B7*ch;* 3 K—R3, Q —R7 *mate.* Culmination of one of the longest and deepest combinations ever seen.

263. *1 . . .* B—Q4*ch;* 2 P —B3, B x P*ch;* 3 R x B, Q—Kt8 *mate.*

264. *1* Q x P*ch,* K x B; 2 R— R4*ch,* K—Kt1; 3 R—R8 *mate.* A familiar theme.

MATE IN THREE MOVES

DIAGRAM 265
Black moves
Black: TARRASCH

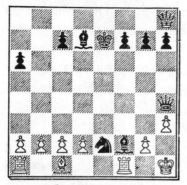

White: AMATEUR
Munich, 1932

DIAGRAM 266
Black moves
Black: COCHRANE

White: POPERT
London, 1841

DIAGRAM 267
White moves
Black: N. BERNSTEIN

White: STEINMEYER
U. S. Open, 1944

DIAGRAM 268
Black moves
Black: KOSTICH

White: ASSIAN
Mexico City, 1930

DIAGRAM 269
White moves
Black: MASON

White: LEONHARDT
London, 1904

DIAGRAM 270
White moves
Black: PARKER

White: PRINS
Elbing, 1945

265. *1 . . .* Q x P*ch;* 2 P x Q, B—B3*ch;* 3 K—R2, B—Kt6 *mate.* Having gobbled two Rooks, White's Queen is not available for defense.

266. *1 . . .* Q x P*ch;* 2 R x Q, R x R*ch;* 3 K—R1, Kt—Kt6 *mate.* White's helplessness is curious.

267. *1* Kt—K5*ch* [1 B—K2*ch* also mates in three], Kt x Q; 2 B—K2*ch,* B—Kt5; 3 B x B *mate.*

268. *1 . . .* R—B7*ch;* 2 K—Kt1 [if 2 K—Q1, Kt—Kt7 *mate*], R—K7*ch;* 3 K—B1, R x Q *mate.* Beautiful cooperation by Black's pieces.

269. *1* Kt—Q8*ch,* K—R1 [if *1 . . .* Kt—Q4 White can mate on the move]; 2 Q—B8*ch* [2 R—K8*ch* is another way], Kt—Kt1; 3 Kt—B7 *mate* or 3 Q x Kt *mate.*

270. *1* R—B6*ch,* K x Kt; 2 P—KKt3!, any; 3 P—R4 *mate.* White's material advantage is decisive in any event, but the text method is the most conclusive.

MATE IN THREE MOVES

DIAGRAM 271
White moves
Black: ROCK

White: STEINITZ
London, 1863

DIAGRAM 272
White moves
Black: STEINER

White: TARTAKOVER
Jurata, 1937

DIAGRAM 273
Black moves
Black: TORRE

White: GRUENFELD
Baden-Baden, 1925

DIAGRAM 274
White moves
Black: KOSTICH

White: TRIFUNOVICH
Rogaska-Slatina, 1937

DIAGRAM 275
White moves
Black: AYERS

White: KAUFMANN
Postal Game, 1944

DIAGRAM 276
White moves
Black: ALMGREN

White: BERLINER
U. S. Open, 1946

271. *1* B—B4*ch*, K—R4; *2* B—Kt4*ch*, K—R5; *3* P x Kt *mate. 1* . . . K—R5 leads to a similar mate. A Queen sacrifice in an Evans produced this one.

272. *1* Q—Kt8*ch*, K—K2; *2* Q—K6*ch*, K—B1; *3* Q—Q6 *mate.*

273. *1* . . . Kt x P*ch*; *2* P x Kt, Q—R3*ch*; *3* B—R3, Q x B *mate.* A possibility completely overlooked by White.

274. *1* Q—R7*ch*, K—B1; *2* B—R6*ch*, Q—Kt2 [if *2* . . . B—Kt2; *3* Q—R8 *mate*]; *3* Q x B *mate.*

275. *1* Q—R6*ch*, K—Kt1; *2* Q—R8*ch*, K—B2; *3* Q—Kt7 *mate.*

276. *1* P—Kt7*ch*, K x P; *2* Kt—R5*ch*, K—R1; *3* R x P *mate.* A Queen sacrifice made this possible.

MATE IN THREE MOVES

DIAGRAM 277
Black moves
Black: NIMZOVICH

White: VIDMAR
New York, 1927

DIAGRAM 278
White moves
Black: PROKES

White: STEINER
Debreczin, 1925

DIAGRAM 279
Black moves
Black: SPIELMANN

White: SCHENKEIN
Vienna, 1910

DIAGRAM 280
Black moves
Black: GOLDBERG

White: MODEL
Leningrad, 1932

DIAGRAM 281
Black moves
Black: RIEMANN

White: ANDERSSEN
Breslau, 1876

DIAGRAM 282
Black moves
Black: BONDAREVSKY

White: KOTOV
Leningrad, 1936

277. *1* . . . Q—Kt5*ch;* 2 K—B2 [or 2 K—R1, Q—B6 *ch;* 3 K—Kt1, Q—B8 *mate*], Q—Kt7*ch;* 3 K—K1, Q—B8 *mate*. White's Queen is far afield.

278. *1* R—Kt8*ch,* K—K2; 2 B—B5*ch,* K—B2; 3 R—B8 *mate*. A mating net with slight material.

279. *1* . . . Q—Q6*ch;* 2 K—B5, P—Kt3*ch;* 3 K—B6, B—Q2 *mate* [or 3 . . . Q—Q2 *mate*]. The end of a typical Spielmann attack!

280. *1* . . . R—R8*ch;* 2 K x R, Q—R3*ch;* 3 K—Kt1, Q—R7 *mate*. An agile Queen.

281. *1* . . . Q x Q*ch;* 2 K x Q, B—B7*ch;* 3 K—B1, R—Q8 *mate*. Black's prosaic first move does the trick.

282. *1* . . . Q x B*ch;* 2 K x Q, B—B4*ch;* 3 K—Q3, Kt x Kt *mate*. It seems almost incredible that this mate occurred in actual play.

MATE IN THREE MOVES

DIAGRAM 283
White moves
Black: HOENLINGER

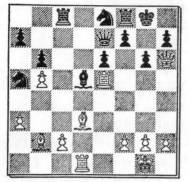

White: SPIELMANN

Match, 1929

DIAGRAM 284
White moves
Black: CARLS

White: HROMADKA

Hamburg, 1910

DIAGRAM 285
White moves
Black: MUHRING

White: SZABO

Zaandam, 1946

DIAGRAM 286
White moves
Black: SALAMON

White: KUENITZ

Tangier, 1907

DIAGRAM 287
Black moves
Black: NIMZOVICH

White: YATES
London, 1927

DIAGRAM 288
Black moves
Black: FLOHR

White: BLECHSCHMIDT
Zwickau, 1930

283. *1* Q x RP*ch!*, K x Q; *2* R—R5*ch*, K—Kt1; *3* R—R8 *mate.* Conclusion of one of Spielmann's finest games.

284. *1* Q—K7*ch*, K—R3 [on *1 . . .* K—Kt1 the mating process is easier, while *1 . . .* K—R1 allows *2* Q—B8 *mate*]; *2* Q—B8*ch*, K x Kt; *3* Q—B4 *mate.*

285. *1* Kt—Kt5*ch*, either P x Kt; *2* R—K7*ch*, K—B1; *3* Q x P *mate.* Just when Black thought he had the Queen trapped!

286. *1* Q x Kt*ch*, P x Q [if *1 . . .* K—K2; *2* B—B5 *mate*]; *2* B x P*ch*, K—K2; *3* B—B5 *mate.*

287. *1 . . .* Kt—K6*ch*; *2* K—Kt1 [or *2* K—R1], Q—B8*ch*; *3* K—R2, Q—Kt7 *mate.*

288. *1 . . .* Q—K5*ch*; *2* K—Kt3, Q—Kt5*ch*; *3* K—R2, R x P *mate.* Conclusion of a remarkably brilliant attack.

MATE IN THREE MOVES

DIAGRAM 289
Black moves
Black: STEINITZ

White: MEITNER
Vienna, 1882

DIAGRAM 290
Black moves
Black: HOLT

White: DREXEL
Miami, 1946

DIAGRAM 291
White moves
Black: CHAJES

White: JANOWSKI
New York, 1916

DIAGRAM 292
White moves
Black: COLLETT

White: BULT
Stockholm, 1946

DIAGRAM 293
White moves
Black: DUNKELBLUM

White: LEMAIRE
Brussels, 1946

DIAGRAM 294
White moves
Black: AMATEUR

White: NAIDORF
Rafaela, 1942

289. *1* . . . R—R8*ch;* 2 B x R [or 2 K—Kt2, R(QR8)—Kt8 *mate*], Q x P*ch;* 3 B—Kt2, Q—Kt8 *mate*. One of Steinitz's rare blindfold games.

290. *1* . . . Kt—Q2; 2 B x Kt, P x B; *3* any, Kt—Kt3 *mate*. A curious finish for actual play. *1* . . . Kt—R5 also mates.

291. *1* P—KR4, R—R1; 2 Q—R7*ch,* R x Q; *3* R x R *mate*. Years later, Mikenas missed this combination in a game with Kashdan.

292. *1* Q—Kt5!, R—KKt1 [if *1* . . . P—Kt3; 2 Q x P *mate*; if *1* . . . P x Kt; 2 Q x P *mate*; if *1* . . . P x Q; 2 R—R3 *mate*]; 2 Q x RP*ch,* P x Q; *3* R x R *mate*.

293. *1* R—Kt8*ch,* Q x R; 2 Q x P*ch,* Q—R2; *3* Q x Q *mate*.

294. *1* R x B, Q x R; 2 Q x P*ch,* Q x Q; *3* Kt—Q7 *mate*. Naidorf's imaginative finish is particularly creditable for a blindfold exhibition.

109

MATE IN THREE MOVES

DIAGRAM 295
White moves
Black: RITZEN

White: ELEKES
Postal Game, 1917

DIAGRAM 296
Black moves
Black: NIMZOVICH

White: GILG
Semmering, 1926

DIAGRAM 297
White moves
Black: KOLISCH

White: MACZUSKY
Paris, 1864

DIAGRAM 298
White moves
Black: SORENSEN

White: JORGENSEN
Storkovenhagen, 1945

DIAGRAM 299
White moves
Black: MAYET

White: LANGE
Berlin, 1853

DIAGRAM 300
White moves
Black: AMATEUR

White: NAIDORF
Buenos Aires, 1942

295. 1 Kt—Kt6*ch*, P x Kt [if *1 . . .* K—Kt1; 2 R—K8*ch*, K—R2; 3 R x R *mate*]; 2 B x P, any; 3 R—K8 *mate.*

296. *1 . . .* B—R6*ch*; 2 Kt x B, Q—B6*ch*; 3 K—Kt1, Q—R8 *mate* or . . . Kt x Kt *mate.*

297. 1 Q—Q8*ch!*, K x Q; 2 B—Kt5*ch*, K—K1; 3 R—Q8 *mate.* The moderns have produced ingenious variations on this theme.

298. 1 Kt—R5*ch*, R x Kt; 2 R x Kt*ch*, K x R; 3 R—K6 *mate.* The position is almost identical with the setting of a problem composed 1000 years ago!!

299. 1 B—B5*ch*, K—B3; 2 Kt—Q8*ch*, K—Q3; 3 B—B4 *mate.* The effectiveness of the minor pieces is impressive.

300. 1 Kt—Q7*ch*, K—K1; 2 Kt—Kt8*ch*, Q x B [or 2 . . . K—B1]; 3 R—Q8 *mate.* Another brilliancy [following a Queen sacrifice] from a simultaneous exhibition.

111

About the Author

FRED REINFELD is the most prolific chess writer in the United States, if not in the world. He has achieved eminence as a player as well as author, and has defeated many of America's leading masters in tournament play. His victims include Reshevsky, Denker, Fine, Horowitz, Lasker, Pinkus, Simonson and the late Frank Marshall. He has won the strong New York State Championship Tournament twice, held the National Intercollegiate title as a youngster and has also won the championship tournaments of our two strongest clubs: the Manhattan and Marshall Chess Clubs.

As a writer, Reinfeld is best known for his encyclopedic knowledge of opening theory (which is buttressed by a fabulously photographic memory), and for his ability to annotate the games of the great masters with such thoroughness, clarity and dramatic appeal that the most complex games of the experts can be completely enjoyed by laymen.

In recent years Reinfeld has devoted considerable attention to the use of the "learning by doing" method, which enables the reader to test and increase his skill. The present volume is an example of this technique, which was also employed in *Chess Mastery By Question and Answer, Chess for Amateurs, Chess Quiz* and *Chess By Yourself.*

CATALOGUE OF DOVER BOOKS

Chess, Checkers, Games, Go

THE ADVENTURE OF CHESS, Edward Lasker. A lively history of chess, from its ancient beginnings in the Indian 4-handed game of Chaturanga, through to the great players of our day, as told by one of America's finest masters. He introduces such unusual sidelights and amusing oddities as Maelzel's chess-playing automaton that beat Napoleon 3 times. Major discussion of chess-playing machines and personal memories of Nimzovich, Capablanca, etc. 5-page chess primer. 11 illustrations, 53 diagrams. 296pp. 5⅜ x 8. S510 Paperbound **$1.75**

A TREASURY OF CHESS LORE, edited by Fred Reinfeld. A delightful collection of anecdotes, short stories, aphorisms by and about the masters, poems, accounts of games and tournaments, photography. Hundreds of humorous, pithy, satirical, wise, and historical episodes, comments, and word portraits. A fascinating "must" for chess players; revealing and perhaps seductive to those who wonder what their friends see in the game. 48 photographs (14 full page plates) 12 diagrams. xi + 306pp. 5⅜ x 8. T458 Paperbound **$1.75**

HOW DO YOU PLAY CHESS? by Fred Reinfeld. A prominent expert covers every basic rule of chess for the beginner in 86 questions and answers: moves, powers of pieces, rationale behind moves, how to play forcefully, history of chess, and much more. Bibliography of chess publications. 11 board diagrams. 48 pages. **FREE**

THE PLEASURES OF CHESS, Assiac. Internationally known British writer, influential chess columnist, writes wittily about wide variety of chess subjects: Anderssen's "Immortal Game;" only game in which both opponents resigned at once; psychological tactics of Reshevsky, Lasker; varieties played by masters for relaxation, such as "losing chess;" sacrificial orgies; etc. These anecdotes, witty observations will give you fresh appreciation of game. 43 problems. 150 diagrams. 139pp. 5⅜ x 8. T597 Paperbound **$1.25**

WIN AT CHESS, F. Reinfeld. 300 practical chess situations from actual tournament play to sharpen your chess eye and test your skill. Traps, sacrifices, mates, winning combinations, subtle exchanges, show you how to WIN AT CHESS. Short notes and tables of solutions and alternative moves help you evaluate your progress. Learn to think ahead playing the "crucial moments" of historic games. 300 diagrams. Notes and solutions. Formerly titled CHESS QUIZ. vi + 120pp. 5⅜ x 8. T438 Paperbound **$1.00**

THE ART OF CHESS, James Mason. An unabridged reprinting of the latest revised edition of the most famous general study of chess ever written. Also included, a complete supplement by Fred Reinfeld, "How Do You Play Chess?", invaluable to beginners for its lively question and answer method. Mason, an early 20th century master, teaches the beginning and intermediate player more than 90 openings, middle game, end game, how to see more moves ahead, to plan purposefully, attack, sacrifice, defend, exchange, and govern general strategy. Supplement. 448 diagrams. 1947 Reinfeld-Bernstein text. Bibliography. xvi + 340pp. 5⅜ x 8. T463 Paperbound **$2.00**

THE PRINCIPLES OF CHESS, James Mason. This "great chess classic" (N. Y. Times) is a general study covering all aspects of the game: basic forces, resistance, obstruction, opposition, relative values, mating, typical end game situations, combinations, much more. The last section discusses openings, with 50 games illustrating modern master play of Rubinstein, Spielmann, Lasker, Capablanca, etc., selected and annotated by Fred Reinfeld. Will improve the game of any intermediate-skilled player, but is so forceful and lucid that an absolute beginner might use it to become an accomplished player. 1946 Reinfeld edition. 166 diagrams. 378pp. 5⅜ x 8. T646 Paperbound **$1.85**

LASKER'S MANUAL OF CHESS, Dr. Emanuel Lasker. Probably the greatest chess player of modern times, Dr. Emanuel Lasker held the world championship 28 years, independent of passing schools or fashions. This unmatched study of the game, chiefly for intermediate to skilled players, analyzes basic methods, combinations, position play, the aesthetics of chess, dozens of different openings, etc., with constant reference to great modern games. Contains a brilliant exposition of Steinitz's important theories. Introduction by Fred Reinfeld. Tables of Lasker's tournament record. 3 indices. 308 diagrams. 1 photograph. xxx + 349pp. 5⅜ x 8. T640 Paperbound **$2.25**

THE ART OF CHESS COMBINATION, E. Znosko-Borovsky. Proves that combinations, perhaps the most aesthetically satisfying, successful technique in chess, can be an integral part of your game, instead of a haphazard occurrence. Games of Capablanca, Rubinstein, Nimzovich, Bird, etc. grouped according to common features, perceptively analyzed to show that every combination begins in certain simple ideas. Will help you to plan many moves ahead. Technical terms almost completely avoided. "In the teaching of chess he may claim to have no superior," P. W. Sergeant. Introduction. Exercises. Solutions. Index. 223pp. 5⅜ x 8. T583 Paperbound **$1.60**

MODERN IDEAS IN CHESS, Richard Reti. An enduring classic, because of its unrivalled explanation of the way master chess had developed in the past hundred years. Reti, who was an outstanding theoretician and player, explains each advance in chess by concentrating on the games of the single master most closely associated with it: Morphy, Anderssen, Steinitz, Lasker, Alekhine, other world champions. Play the games in this volume, study Reti's perceptive observations, and have a living picture of the road chess has travelled. Introduction. 34 diagrams. 192pp. 5⅜ x 8. **T638 Paperbound $1.25**

THE BOOK OF THE NEW YORK INTERNATIONAL CHESS TOURNAMENT, 1924, annotated by A. Alekhine and edited by H. Helms. Long a rare collector's item, this is the book of one of the most brilliant tournaments of all time, during which Capablanca, Lasker, Alekhine, Reti, and others immeasurably enriched chess theory in a thrilling contest. All 110 games played, with Alekhine's unusually penetrating notes. 15 photographs. xi + 271pp. 5⅜ x 8. **T752 Paperbound $1.85**

KERES' BEST GAMES OF CHESS, selected, annotated by F. Reinfeld. 90 best games, 1931-1948, by one of boldest, most exciting players of modern chess. Games against Alekhine, Bogolyubov, Capablanca, Euwe, Fine, Reshevsky, other masters, show his treatments of openings such as Giuoco Piano, Alekhine Defense, Queen's Gambit Declined; attacks, sacrifices, alternative methods. Preface by Keres gives personal glimpses, evaluations of rivals. 110 diagrams. 272pp. 5⅜ x 8. **T593 Paperbound $1.35**

HYPERMODERN CHESS as developed in the games of its greatest exponent, ARON NIMZOVICH, edited by Fred Reinfeld. An intensely original player and analyst, Nimzovich's extraordinary approaches startled and often angered the chess world. This volume, designed for the average player, shows in his victories over Alekhine, Lasker, Marshall, Rubinstein, Spielmann, and others, how his iconoclastic methods infused new life into the game. Use Nimzovich to invigorate your play and startle opponents. Introduction. Indices of players and openings. 180 diagrams. viii + 220pp. 5⅜ x 8. **T448 Paperbound $1.50**

THE DEVELOPMENT OF A CHESS GENIUS: 100 INSTRUCTIVE GAMES OF ALEKHINE, F. Reinfeld. 100 games of the chess giant's formative years, 1905-1914, from age 13 to maturity, each annotated and commented upon by Fred Reinfeld. Included are matches against Bogolyubov, Capablanca, Tarrasch, and many others. You see the growth of an inexperienced genius into one of the greatest players of all time. Many of these games have never appeared before in book form. "One of America's most significant contributions to the chess world," Chess Life. New introduction. Index of players, openings. 204 illustrations. xv +227pp. 5¾ x 8. **T551 Paperbound $1.35**

RESHEVSKY'S BEST GAMES OF CHESS, Samuel Reshevsky. One time 4-year-old chess genius, 5-time winner U. S. Chess Championship, selects, annotates 110 of his best games, illustrating theories, favorite methods of play against Capablanca, Alekhine, Bogolyubov, Kashdan, Vidmar, Botvinnik, others. Clear, non-technical style. Personal impressions of opponents, autobiographical material, tournament match record. Formerly "Reshevsky on Chess." 309 diagrams, 2 photos. 288pp. 5⅜ x 8. **T606 Paperbound $1.25**

ONE HUNDRED SELECTED GAMES, Mikhail Botvinnik. Author's own choice of his best games before becoming World Champion in 1948, beginning with first big tournament, the USSR Championship, 1927. Shows his great power of analysis as he annotates these games, giving strategy, technique against Alekhine, Capablanca, Euwe, Keres, Reshevsky, Smyslov, Vidmar, many others. Discusses his career, methods of play, system of training. 6 studies of endgame positions. 221 diagrams. 272pp. 5⅜ x 8. **T620 Paperbound $1.50**

RUBINSTEIN'S CHESS MASTERPIECES, selected, annotated by Hans Kmoch. Thoroughgoing mastery of opening, middle game; faultless technique in endgame, particularly rook and pawn endings; ability to switch from careful positional play to daring combinations; all distinguish the play of Rubinstein. 100 best games, against Janowski, Nimzowitch, Tarrasch, Vidmar, Capablanca, other greats, carefully annotated, will improve your game rapidly. Biographical introduction, B. F. Winkelman. 103 diagrams. 192pp. 5⅜ x 8. **T617 Paperbound $1.25**

TARRASCH'S BEST GAMES OF CHESS, selected & annotated by Fred Reinfeld. First definitive collection of games by Siegbert Tarrasch, winner of 7 international tournaments, and the leading theorist of classical chess. 183 games cover fifty years of play against Mason, Mieses, Paulsen, Teichmann, Pillsbury, Janowski, others. Reinfeld includes Tarrasch's own analyses of many of these games. A careful study and replaying of the games will give you a sound understanding of classical methods, and many hours of enjoyment. Introduction. Indexes. 183 diagrams. xxiv + 386pp. 5⅜ x 8. **T644 Paperbound $2.00**

MARSHALL'S BEST GAMES OF CHESS, F. J. Marshall. Grandmaster, U. S. Champion for 27 years, tells story of career; presents magnificent collection of 140 of best games, annotated by himself. Games against Alekhine, Capablanca, Emanuel Lasker, Janowski, Rubinstein, Pillsbury, etc. Special section analyzes openings such as King's Gambit, Ruy Lopez, Alekhine's Defense, Giuoco Piano, others. A study of Marshall's brilliant offensives, slashing attacks, extraordinary sacrifices, will rapidly improve your game. Formerly "My Fifty Years of Chess." Introduction. 19 diagrams. 13 photos. 250pp. 5⅜ x 8. **T604 Paperbound $1.45**

CATALOGUE OF DOVER BOOKS

THE HASTINGS CHESS TOURNAMENT, 1895, edited by Horace F. Cheshire. This is the complete tournament book of the famous Hastings 1895 tournament. One of the most exciting tournaments ever to take place, it evoked the finest play from such players as Dr. Lasker, Steinitz, Tarrasch, Harry Pillsbury, Mason, Tchigorin, Schlecter, and others. It was not only extremely exciting as an event, it also created first-rate chess. This book contains fully annotated all 230 games, full information about the playing events, biographies of the players, and much other material that makes it a chess classic. 22 photos, 174 diagrams. x + 370pp. 5⅝ x 8½.   T288 Paperbound **$2.00**

THE BOOK OF THE NOTTINGHAM INTERNATIONAL CHESS TOURNAMENT, 1936, Annotated by Dr. Alexander Alekhine. The Nottingham 1936 tournament is regarded by many chess enthusiasts as the greatest tournament of recent years. It brought together all the living former world champions, the current chess champion, and the future world champion: Dr. Lasker, Capablanca, Alekhine, Euwe, Botvinnik, and Reshevsky, Fine, Flohr, Tartakover, Vidmar, and Bogoljubov. The play was brilliant throughout. This volume contains all 105 of the games played, provided with the remarkable annotations of Alekhine. 1 illustration, 121 diagrams. xx + 291pp. 5⅜ x 8½.   T189 Paperbound **$2.00**

CHESS FOR FUN AND CHESS FOR BLOOD, Edward Lasker. A genial, informative book by one of century's leading masters. Incisive comments on chess as a form of art and recreation, on how a master prepares for and plays a tournament. Best of all is author's move-by-move analysis of his game with Dr. Emanuel Lasker in 1924 World Tournament, a charming and thorough recreation of one of the great games in history: the author's mental processes; how his calculations were upset; how both players blundered; the surprising outcome. Who could not profit from this study-in-depth? For the enthusiast who likes to read about chess as well as play it. Corrected (1942) edition. Preface contains 8 letters to author about the fun of chess. 95 illustrations by Maximilian Mopp. 224pp. 5⅜ x 8½.   T146 Paperbound **$1.25**

HOW NOT TO PLAY CHESS, Eugene A. Znosko-Borovsky. Sticking to a few well-chosen examples and explaining every step along the way, an outstanding chess expositor shows how to avoid playing a hit-or-miss game and instead develop general plans of action based on positional analysis: weak and strong squares, the notion of the controlled square, how to seize control of open lines, weak points in the pawn structure, and so on. Definition and illustration of typical chess mistakes plus 20 problems (from master games) added by Fred Reinfeld for the 1949 edition and a number of good-to-memorize tips make this a lucid book that can teach in a few hours what might otherwise take years to learn. 119pp. 5⅜ x 8.   T920 Paperbound **$1.00**

THE SOVIET SCHOOL OF CHESS, A. Kotov and M. Yudovich. 128 master games, most unavailable elsewhere, by 51 outstanding players, including Botvinnik, Keres, Smyslov, Tal, against players like Capablanca, Euwe, Reshevsky. All carefully annotated, analyzed. Valuable biographical information about each player, early history of Russian chess, careers and contributions of Chigorin and Alekhine, development of Soviet school from 1920 to present with full over-all study of main features of its games, history of Russian chess literature. The most comprehensive work on Russian chess ever printed, the richest single sourcebook for up-to-date Russian theory and strategy. New introduction. Appendix of Russian Grandmasters, Masters, Master Composers. Two indexes (Players, Games). 30 photographs. 182 diagrams. vi + 390pp. 5⅜ x 8.   T26 Paperbound **$2.00**

THE ART OF THE CHECKMATE, Georges Renaud and Victor Kahn. Two former national chess champions of France examine 127 games, identify 23 kinds of mate, and show the rationale for each. These include Legal's pseudo sacrifice, the double check, the smothered mate, Greco's mate, Morphy's mate, the mate of two bishops, two knights, many, many more. Analysis of ideas, not memorization problems. Review quizzes with answers help readers gauge progress. 80 quiz examples and solutions. 299 diagrams. vi + 208pp.   T106 Paperbound **$1.35**

HOW TO SOLVE CHESS PROBLEMS, K. S. Howard. Full of practical suggestions for the fan or the beginner—who knows only the moves of the chessmen. Contains preliminary section and 58 two-move, 46 three-move, and 8 four-move problems composed by 27 outstanding American problem creators in the last 30 years. Explanation of all terms and exhaustive index. "Just what is wanted for the student," Brian Harley. 112 problems, solutions. vi +171pp. 5⅜ x 8.   T748 Paperbound **$1.00**

CHESS STRATEGY, Edward Lasker. Keres, Fine, and other great players have acknowledged their debt to this book, which has taught just about the whole modern school how to play forcefully and intelligently. Covers fundamentals, general strategic principles, middle and end game, objects of attack, etc. Includes 48 dramatic games from master tournaments, all fully analyzed. "Best textbook I know in English," J. R. Capablanca. New introduction by author. Table of openings. Index. 167 illustrations. vii + 282pp. 5⅜ x 8.   T528 Paperbound **$1.65**

REINFELD ON THE END GAME IN CHESS, F. Reinfeld. Formerly titled PRACTICAL END-GAME PLAY, this book contains clear, simple analyses of 62 end games by such masters as Alekhine, Tarrasch, Marshall, Morphy, Capablanca, and many others. Primary emphasis is on the general principles of transition from middle play to end play. This book is unusual in analyzing weak or incorrect moves to show how error occurs and how to avoid it. Covers king and pawn, minor piece, queen endings, weak squares, centralization, tempo moves, and many other vital factors. 62 diagrams. vi + 177pp. 5⅜ x 8.   T417 Paperbound **$1.25**

THE AMERICAN TWO-MOVE CHESS PROBLEM, Kenneth S. Howard. One of this country's foremost contemporary problem composers selects an interesting, diversified collection of the best two-movers by 58 top American composers. Involving complete blocks, mutates, line openings and closings, other unusual moves, these problems will help almost any player improve his strategic approach. Probably has no equal for all around artistic excellence, surprising keymoves, interesting strategy. Includes 30-page history of development of American two-mover from Loyd, its founder, to the present. Index of composers. vii + 99pp. 5⅜ x 8½.
T997 Paperbound **$1.00**

WIN AT CHECKERS, M. Hopper. (Formerly CHECKERS). The former World's Unrestricted Checker Champion discusses the principles of the game, expert's shots and traps, problems for the beginner, standard openings, locating your best move, the end game, opening "blitzkrieg" moves, ways to draw when you are behind your opponent, etc. More than 100 detailed questions and answers anticipate your problems. Appendix. 75 problems with solutions and diagrams. Index. 79 figures. xi + 107pp. 5⅜ x 8.
T363 Paperbound **$1.00**

GAMES ANCIENT AND ORIENTAL, AND HOW TO PLAY THEM, E. Falkener. A connoisseur's selection of exciting and different games: Oriental varieties of chess, with unusual pieces and moves (including Japanese shogi); the original pachisi; go; reconstructions of lost Roman and Egyptian games; and many more. Full rules and sample games. Now play at home the games that have entertained millions, not on a fad basis, but for millennia. 345 illustrations and figures. iv + 366pp. 5⅜ x 8.
T739 Paperbound **$2.00**

GO AND GO-MOKU, Edward Lasker. A fascinating Oriental game, Go, is winning new devotees in America daily. Rules that you can learn in a few minutes—a wealth of combinations that makes it more profound than chess! This is an easily followed step-by-step explanation of this 2000-year-old game, beginning with fundamentals. New chapter on advanced strategy in this edition! Also contains rules for Go-Moku, a very easy sister game. 72 diagrams. xix + 215pp. 5⅜ x 8.
T613 Paperbound **$1.50**

HOW TO FORCE CHECKMATE, F. Reinfeld. Formerly titled CHALLENGE TO CHESSPLAYERS, this is an invaluable collection of 300 lightning strokes selected from actual masters' play, which will demonstrate how to smash your opponent's game with strong decisive moves. No board needed — clear, practical diagrams and easy-to-understand solutions. Learn to plan up to three moves ahead and play a superior end game. 300 diagrams. 111pp. 5⅜ x 8.
T439 Paperbound **$1.25**

CHESSBOARD MAGIC! A COLLECTION OF 160 BRILLIANT ENDINGS, I. Chernev. Contains 160 endgame compositions, all illustrating not only ingenuity of composition, but inherent beauty of solution. In one, five Knights are needed to force mate; in another White forces stalemate though Black finishes eight passed pawns ahead; 150 more, all remarkable, all will sharpen your imagination and increase your skill. "Inexhaustible source of entertainment, an endless feast of delight," Reuben Fine, Grandmaster. Introduction. 160 diagrams. Index of composers. vii + 172pp. 5⅜ x 8.
T607 Paperbound **$1.00**

LEARN CHESS FROM THE MASTERS, F. Reinfeld. Formerly titled CHESS BY YOURSELF, this book contains 10 games which you play against such masters as Marshall, Bronstein, Najdorf, and others, and an easy system for grading each move you make against a variety of other possible moves. Detailed annotations reveal the principles of the game through actual play. 91 diagrams. viii + 144pp. 5⅜ x 8.
T362 Paperbound **$1.00**

MORPHY'S GAMES OF CHESS, edited by Philip W. Sergeant. You can put boldness into your game by following the brilliant, forceful moves of the man who has been called the greatest chess player of all time. Here are 300 of Morphy's best games carefully annotated to reveal Morphy's principles. 54 classics against masters like Anderssen, Harrwitz, Bird, Paulsen, and others. 52 games at odds; 54 blindfold games; plus over 100 others. Unabridged reissue of the latest revised edition. Bibliography. New introduction by Fred Reinfeld. Annotations and introduction by Sergeant. Index. 235 diagrams. x + 352pp. 5⅜ x 8. T386 Paperbound **$1.85**

CHESS PRAXIS, Aron Nimzovich. Nimzovich was the stormy petrel of chess in the first decades of this century, and his system, known as hypermodern chess, revolutionized all play since his time. Casting aside the classical chess theory of Steinitz and Tarrasch, he created his own analysis of chess, considering dynamic patterns as they emerge during play. This is the fullest exposition of his ideas, and it is easily one of the dozen greatest books ever written on chess. Nimzovich illustrates each of his principles with at least two games, and shows how he applied his concepts successfully in games against such masters as Alekhine, Tarrasch, Reti, Rubinstein, Capablanca, Spielmann and others. Indispensable to every serious chess player. Translated by J. DuMont. 135 diagrams, 1 photo. xi + 364pp. 5½ x 8⅝.
T296 Paperbound **$2.25**

CHESS AND CHECKERS: THE WAY TO MASTERSHIP, Edward Lasker. Complete, lucid instructions for the beginner—and valuable suggestions for the advanced player! For both games the great master and teacher presents fundamentals, elementary tactics, and steps toward becoming a superior player. He concentrates on general principles rather than a mass of rules, comprehension rather than brute memory. Historical introduction. 118 diagrams. xiv + 167pp. 5⅜ x 8.
T657 Paperbound **$1.15**

Puzzles, Mathematical Recreations

SYMBOLIC LOGIC and THE GAME OF LOGIC, Lewis Carroll. "Symbolic Logic" is not concerned with modern symbolic logic, but is instead a collection of over 380 problems posed with charm and imagination, using the syllogism, and a fascinating diagrammatic method of drawing conclusions. In "The Game of Logic" Carroll's whimsical imagination devises a logical game played with 2 diagrams and counters (included) to manipulate hundreds of tricky syllogisms. The final section, "Hit or Miss" is a lagniappe of 101 additional puzzles in the delightful Carroll manner. Until this reprint edition, both of these books were rarities costing up to $15 each. Symbolic Logic: Index. xxxi + 199pp. The Game of Logic: 96pp. 2 vols. bound as one. 5⅜ x 8. **T492 Paperbound $1.50**

PILLOW PROBLEMS and A TANGLED TALE, Lewis Carroll. One of the rarest of all Carroll's works, "Pillow Problems" contains 72 original math puzzles, all typically ingenious. Particularly fascinating are Carroll's answers which remain exactly as he thought them out, reflecting his actual mental process. The problems in "A Tangled Tale" are in story form, originally appearing as a monthly magazine serial. Carroll not only gives the solutions, but uses answers sent in by readers to discuss wrong approaches and misleading paths, and grades them for insight. Both of these books were rarities until this edition, "Pillow Problems" costing up to $25, and "A Tangled Tale" $15. Pillow Problems: Preface and Introduction by Lewis Carroll. xx + 109pp. A Tangled Tale: 6 illustrations. 152pp. Two vols. bound as one. 5⅜ x 8. **T493 Paperbound $1.50**

AMUSEMENTS IN MATHEMATICS, Henry Ernest Dudeney. The foremost British originator of mathematical puzzles is always intriguing, witty, and paradoxical in this classic, one of the largest collections of mathematical amusements. More than 430 puzzles, problems, and paradoxes. Mazes and games, problems on number manipulation, unicursal and other route problems, puzzles on measuring, weighing, packing, age, kinship, chessboards, joiners', crossing river, plane figure dissection, and many others. Solutions. More than 450 illustrations. vii + 258pp. 5⅜ x 8. **T473 Paperbound $1.25**

THE CANTERBURY PUZZLES, Henry Dudeney. Chaucer's pilgrims set one another problems in story form. Also Adventures of the Puzzle Club, the Strange Escape of the King's Jester, the Monks of Riddlewell, the Squire's Christmas Puzzle Party, and others. All puzzles are original, based on dissecting plane figures, arithmetic, algebra, elementary calculus and other branches of mathematics, and purely logical ingenuity. "The limit of ingenuity and intricacy," The Observer. Over 110 puzzles. Full Solutions. 150 illustrations. vii + 225pp. 5⅜ x 8. **T474 Paperbound $1.25**

MATHEMATICAL EXCURSIONS, H. A. Merrill. Even if you hardly remember your high school math, you'll enjoy the 90 stimulating problems contained in this book and you will come to understand a great many mathematical principles with surprisingly little effort. Many useful shortcuts and diversions not generally known are included: division by inspection, Russian peasant multiplication, memory systems for pi, building odd and even magic squares, square roots by geometry, dyadic systems, and many more. Solutions to difficult problems. 50 illustrations. 145pp. 5⅜ x 8. **T350 Paperbound $1.00**

MAGIC SQUARES AND CUBES, W. S. Andrews. Only book-length treatment in English, a thorough non-technical description and analysis. Here are nasik, overlapping, pandiagonal, serrated squares; magic circles, cubes, spheres, rhombuses. Try your hand at 4-dimensional magical figures! Much unusual folklore and tradition included. High school algebra is sufficient. 754 diagrams and illustrations. viii + 419pp. 5⅜ x 8. **T658 Paperbound $1.85**

CALIBAN'S PROBLEM BOOK: MATHEMATICAL, INFERENTIAL AND CRYPTOGRAPHIC PUZZLES, H. Phillips (Caliban), S. T. Shovelton, G. S. Marshall. 105 ingenious problems by the greatest living creator of puzzles based on logic and inference. Rigorous, modern, piquant; reflecting their author's unusual personality, these intermediate and advanced puzzles all involve the ability to reason clearly through complex situations; some call for mathematical knowledge, ranging from algebra to number theory. Solutions. xi + 180pp. 5⅜ x 8.
T736 Paperbound $1.25

MATHEMATICAL PUZZLES FOR BEGINNERS AND ENTHUSIASTS, G. Mott-Smith. 188 mathematical puzzles based on algebra, dissection of plane figures, permutations, and probability, that will test and improve your powers of inference and interpretation. The Odic Force, The Spider's Cousin, Ellipse Drawing, theory and strategy of card and board games like tit-tat-toe, go moku, salvo, and many others. 100 pages of detailed mathematical explanations. Appendix of primes, square roots, etc. 135 illustrations. 2nd revised edition. 248pp. 5⅜ x 8.
T198 Paperbound $1.00

MATHEMAGIC, MAGIC PUZZLES, AND GAMES WITH NUMBERS, R. V. Heath. More than 60 new puzzles and stunts based on the properties of numbers. Easy techniques for multiplying large numbers mentally, revealing hidden numbers magically, finding the date of any day in any year, and dozens more. Over 30 pages devoted to magic squares, triangles, cubes, circles, etc. Edited by J. S. Meyer. 76 illustrations. 128pp. 5⅜ x 8. **T110 Paperbound $1.00**

MATHEMATICAL RECREATIONS, M. Kraitchik. One of the most thorough compilations of unusual mathematical problems for beginners and advanced mathematicians. Historical problems from Greek, Medieval, Arabic, Hindu sources. 50 pages devoted to pastimes derived from figurate numbers, Mersenne numbers, Fermat numbers, primes and probability. 40 pages of magic, Euler, Latin, panmagic squares. 25 new positional and permutational games of permanent value: fairy chess, latruncles, reversi, jinx, ruma, lasca, tricolor, tetrachrome, etc. Complete rigorous solutions. Revised second edition. 181 illustrations. 333pp. 5⅜ x 8.
T163 Paperbound **$1.75**

MATHEMATICAL PUZZLES OF SAM LOYD, selected and edited by M. Gardner. Choice puzzles by the greatest American puzzle creator and innovator. Selected from his famous collection, "Cyclopedia of Puzzles," they retain the unique style and historical flavor of the originals. There are posers based on arithmetic, algebra, probability, game theory, route tracing, topology, counter, sliding block, operations research, geometrical dissection. Includes the famous "14-15" puzzle which was a national craze, and his "Horse of a Different Color" which sold millions of copies. 117 of his most ingenious puzzles in all, 120 line drawings and diagrams. Solutions. Selected references. xx + 167pp. 5⅜ x 8. T498 Paperbound **$1.00**

MATHEMATICAL PUZZLES OF SAM LOYD, Vol. II, selected and edited by Martin Gardner. The outstanding 2nd selection from the great American innovator's "Cyclopedia of Puzzles": speed and distance problems, clock problems, plane and solid geometry, calculus problems, etc. Analytical table of contents that groups the puzzles according to the type of mathematics necessary to solve them. 166 puzzles, 150 original line drawings and diagrams. Selected references. xiv + 177pp. 5⅜ x 8. T709 Paperbound **$1.00**

ARITHMETICAL EXCURSIONS: AN ENRICHMENT OF ELEMENTARY MATHEMATICS, H. Bowers and J. Bowers. A lively and lighthearted collection of facts and entertainments for anyone who enjoys manipulating numbers or solving arithmetical puzzles: methods of arithmetic never taught in school, little-known facts about the most simple numbers, and clear explanations of more sophisticated topics; mysteries and folklore of numbers, the "Hin-dog-abic" number system, etc. First publication. Index. 529 numbered problems and diversions, all with answers. Bibliography. 60 figures. xiv + 320pp. 5⅜ x 8. T770 Paperbound **$1.65**

CRYPTANALYSIS, H. F. Gaines. Formerly entitled ELEMENTARY CRYPTANALYSIS, this introductory-intermediate level text is the best book in print on cryptograms and their solution. It covers all major techniques of the past, and contains much that is not generally known except to experts. Full details about concealment, substitution, and transposition ciphers; periodic mixed alphabets, multafid, Kasiski and Vigenere methods, Ohaver patterns, Playfair, and scores of other topics. 6 language letter and word frequency appendix. 167 problems, now furnished with solutions. Index. 173 figures. vi + 230pp. 5⅜ x 8.
T97 Paperbound **$2.00**

CRYPTOGRAPHY, L. D. Smith. An excellent introductory work on ciphers and their solution, the history of secret writing, and actual methods and problems in such techniques as transposition and substitution. Appendices describe the enciphering of Japanese, the Baconian biliteral cipher, and contain frequency tables and a bibliography for further study. Over 150 problems with solutions. 160pp. 5⅜ x 8. T247 Paperbound **$1.00**

PUZZLE QUIZ AND STUNT FUN, J. Meyer. The solution to party doldrums. 238 challenging puzzles, stunts and tricks. Mathematical puzzles like The Clever Carpenter, Atom Bomb; mysteries and deductions like The Bridge of Sighs, The Nine Pearls, Dog Logic; observation puzzles like Cigarette Smokers, Telephone Dial; over 200 others including magic squares, tongue twisters, puns, anagrams, and many others. All problems solved fully. 250pp. 5⅜ x 8.
T337 Paperbound **$1.00**

101 PUZZLES IN THOUGHT AND LOGIC, C. R. Wylie, Jr. Brand new problems you need no special knowledge to solve! Take the kinks out of your mental "muscles" and enjoy solving murder problems, the detection of lying fishermen, the logical identification of color by a blindman, and dozens more. Introduction with simplified explanation of general scientific method and puzzle solving. 128pp. 5⅜ x 8. T367 Paperbound **$1.00**

MY BEST PROBLEMS IN MATHEMATICS, Hubert Phillips ("Caliban"). Only elementary mathematics needed to solve these 100 witty, catchy problems by a master problem creator. Problems on the odds in cards and dice, problems in geometry, algebra, permutations, even problems that require no math at all—just a logical mind, clear thinking. Solutions completely worked out. If you enjoy mysteries, alerting your perceptive powers and exercising your detective's eye, you'll find these cryptic puzzles a challenging delight. Original 1961 publication. 100 puzzles, solutions. x + 107pp. 5⅝ x 8. T91 Paperbound **$1.00**

MY BEST PUZZLES IN LOGIC AND REASONING, Hubert Phillips ("Caliban"). A new collection of 100 inferential and logical puzzles chosen from the best that have appeared in England, available for first time in U.S. By the most endlessly resourceful puzzle creator now living. All data presented are both necessary and sufficient to allow a single unambiguous answer. No special knowledge is required for problems ranging from relatively simple to completely original one-of-a-kinds. Guaranteed to please beginners and experts of all ages. Original publication. 100 puzzles, full solutions. x + 107pp. 5⅜ x 8. T119 Paperbound **$1.00**

THE BOOK OF MODERN PUZZLES, G. L. Kaufman. A completely new series of puzzles as fascinating as crossword and deduction puzzles but based upon different principles and techniques. Simple 2-minute teasers, word labyrinths, design and pattern puzzles, logic and observation puzzles — over 150 braincrackers. Answers to all problems. 116 illustrations. 192pp. 5⅜ x 8.
.T143 Paperbound **$1.00**

NEW WORD PUZZLES, G. L. Kaufman. 100 ENTIRELY NEW puzzles based on words and their combinations that will delight crossword puzzle, Scrabble and Jotto fans. Chess words, based on the moves of the chess king; design-onyms, symmetrical designs made of synonyms; rhymed double-crostics; syllable sentences; addle letter anagrams; alphagrams; linkograms; and many others all brand new. Full solutions. Space to work problems. 196 figures. vi + 122pp. 5⅜ x 8.
T344 Paperbound **$1.00**

MAZES AND LABYRINTHS: A BOOK OF PUZZLES, W. Shepherd. Mazes, formerly associated with mystery and ritual, are still among the most intriguing of intellectual puzzles. This is a novel and different collection of 50 amusements that embody the principle of the maze: mazes in the classical tradition; 3-dimensional, ribbon, and Möbius-strip mazes; hidden messages; spatial arrangements; etc.—almost all built on amusing story situations. 84 illustrations. Essay on maze psychology. Solutions. xv + 122pp. 5⅜ x 8.
T731 Paperbound **$1.00**

MAGIC TRICKS & CARD TRICKS, W. Jonson. Two books bound as one. 52 tricks with cards, 37 tricks with coins, bills, eggs, smoke, ribbons, slates, etc. Details on presentation, misdirection, and routining will help you master such famous tricks as the Changing Card, Card in the Pocket, Four Aces, Coin Through the Hand, Bill in the Egg, Afghan Bands, and over 75 others. If you follow the lucid exposition and key diagrams carefully, you will finish these two books with an astonishing mastery of magic. 106 figures. 224pp. 5⅜ x 8. T909 Paperbound **$1.00**

PANORAMA OF MAGIC, Milbourne Christopher. A profusely illustrated history of stage magic, a unique selection of prints and engravings from the author's private collection of magic memorabilia, the largest of its kind. Apparatus, stage settings and costumes; ingenious apparatus distributed by the performers and satiric broadsides passed around in the streets ridiculing pompous showmen; programs; decorative souvenirs. The lively text, by one of America's foremost professional magicians, is full of anecdotes about almost legendary wizards: Dede, the Egyptian; Philadelphia, the wonder-worker; Robert-Houdin, "the father of modern magic;" Harry Houdini; scores more. Altogether a pleasure package for anyone interested in magic, stage setting and design, ethnology, psychology, or simply in unusual people. A Dover original. 295 illustrations; 8 in full color. Index. viii + 216pp. 8⅜ x 11¼.
T774 Paperbound **$2.25**

HOUDINI ON MAGIC, Harry Houdini. One of the greatest magicians of modern times explains his most prized secrets. How locks are picked, with illustrated picks and skeleton keys; how a girl is sawed into twins; how to walk through a brick wall — Houdini's explanations of 44 stage tricks with many diagrams. Also included is a fascinating discussion of great magicians of the past and the story of his fight against fraudulent mediums and spiritualists. Edited by W.B. Gibson and M.N. Young. Bibliography. 155 figures, photos. xv + 280pp. 5⅜ x 8.
T384 Paperbound **$1.35**

MATHEMATICS, MAGIC AND MYSTERY, Martin Gardner. Why do card tricks work? How do magicians perform astonishing mathematical feats? How is stage mind-reading possible? This is the first book length study explaining the application of probability, set theory, theory of numbers, topology, etc., to achieve many startling tricks. Non-technical, accurate, detailed! 115 sections discuss tricks with cards, dice, coins, knots, geometrical vanishing illusions, how a Curry square "demonstrates" that the sum of the parts may be greater than the whole, and dozens of others. No sleight of hand necessary! 135 illustrations. xii + 174pp. 5⅜ x 8.
T335 Paperbound **$1.00**

EASY-TO-DO ENTERTAINMENTS AND DIVERSIONS WITH COINS, CARDS, STRING, PAPER AND MATCHES, R. M. Abraham. Over 300 tricks, games and puzzles will provide young readers with absorbing fun. Sections on card games; paper-folding; tricks with coins, matches and pieces of string; games for the agile; toy-making from common household objects; mathematical recreations; and 50 miscellaneous pastimes. Anyone in charge of groups of youngsters, including hard-pressed parents, and in need of suggestions on how to keep children sensibly amused and quietly content will find this book indispensable. Clear, simple text, copious number of delightful line drawings and illustrative diagrams. Originally titled "Winter Nights Entertainments." Introduction by Lord Baden Powell. 329 illustrations. v + 186pp. 5⅜ x 8½.
T921 Paperbound **$1.00**

STRING FIGURES AND HOW TO MAKE THEM, Caroline Furness Jayne. 107 string figures plus variations selected from the best primitive and modern examples developed by Navajo, Apache, pygmies of Africa, Eskimo, in Europe, Australia, China, etc. The most readily understandable, easy-to-follow book in English on perennially popular recreation. Crystal-clear exposition; step-by-step diagrams. Everyone from kindergarten children to adults looking for unusual diversion will be endlessly amused. Index. Bibliography. Introduction by A. C. Haddon. 17 full-page plates. 960 illustrations. xxiii + 401pp. 5⅜ x 8½.
T152 Paperbound **$2.00**

New Books

101 PATCHWORK PATTERNS, Ruby Short McKim. With no more ability than the fundamentals of ordinary sewing, you will learn to make over 100 beautiful quilts: flowers, rainbows, Irish chains, fish and bird designs, leaf designs, unusual geometric patterns, many others. Cutting designs carefully diagrammed and described, suggestions for materials, yardage estimates, step-by-step instructions, plus entertaining stories of origins of quilt names, other folklore. Revised 1962. 101 full-sized patterns. 140 illustrations. Index. 128pp. 7⅞ x 10¾.
T773 Paperbound **$1.85**

ESSENTIAL GRAMMAR SERIES
By concentrating on the essential core of material that constitutes the semantically most important forms and areas of a language and by stressing explanation (often bringing parallel English forms into the discussion) rather than rote memory, this new series of grammar books is among the handiest language aids ever devised. Designed by linguists and teachers for adults with limited learning objectives and learning time, these books omit nothing important, yet they teach more usable language material and do it more quickly and permanently than any other self-study material. Clear and rigidly economical, they concentrate upon immediately usable language material, logically organized so that related material is always presented together. Any reader of typical capability can use them to refresh his grasp of language, to supplement self-study language records or conventional grammars used in schools, or to begin language study on his own. Now available:

ESSENTIAL GERMAN GRAMMAR, Dr. Guy Stern & E. F. Bleiler. Index. Glossary of terms. 128pp. 5⅜ x 8.
T422 Paperbound **$1.00**

ESSENTIAL FRENCH GRAMMAR, Dr. Seymour Resnick. Index. Cognate list. Glossary. 159pp. 5⅜ x 8.
T419 Paperbound **$1.00**

ESSENTIAL ITALIAN GRAMMAR, Dr. Olga Ragusa. Index. Glossary. 111pp. 5⅜ x 8.
T779 Paperbound **$1.00**

ESSENTIAL SPANISH GRAMMAR, Dr. Seymour Resnick. Index. 50-page cognate list. Glossary. 138pp. 5⅜ x 8.
T780 Paperbound **$1.00**

PHILOSOPHIES OF MUSIC HISTORY: A Study of General Histories of Music, 1600-1960, Warren D. Allen. Unquestionably one of the most significant documents yet to appear in musicology, this thorough survey covers the entire field of historical research in music. An influential masterpiece of scholarship, it includes early music histories; theories on the ethos of music; lexicons, dictionaries and encyclopedias of music; musical historiography through the centuries; philosophies of music history; scores of related topics. Copiously documented. New preface brings work up to 1960. Index. 317-item bibliography. 9 illustrations; 3 full-page plates. 5⅜ x 8½. xxxiv + 382pp.
T282 Paperbound **$2.00**

MR. DOOLEY ON IVRYTHING AND IVRYBODY, Finley Peter Dunne. The largest collection in print of hilarious utterances by the irrepressible Irishman of Archey Street, one of the most vital characters in American fiction. Gathered from the half dozen books that appeared during the height of Mr. Dooley's popularity, these 102 pieces are all unaltered and uncut, and they are all remarkably fresh and pertinent even today. Selected and edited by Robert Hutchinson. 5⅜ x 8½. xii + 244p.
T626 Paperbound **$1.00**

TREATISE ON PHYSIOLOGICAL OPTICS, Hermann von Helmholtz. Despite new investigations, this important work will probably remain preeminent. Contains everything known about physiological optics up to 1925, covering scores of topics under the general headings of dioptrics of the eye, sensations of vision, and perecptions of vision. Von Helmholtz's voluminous data are all included, as are extensive supplementary matter incorporated into the third German edition, new material prepared for 1925 English edition, and copious textual annotations by J. P. C. Southall. The most exhaustive treatise ever prepared on the subject, it has behind it a list of contributors that will never again be duplicated. Translated and edited by J. P. C. Southall. Bibliography. Indexes. 312 illustrations. 3 volumes bound as 2. Total of 1749pp. 5⅜ x 8.
S15-16 Two volume set, Clothbound **$15.00**

THE ARTISTIC ANATOMY OF TREES, Rex Vicat Cole. Even the novice with but an elementary knowledge of drawing and none of the structure of trees can learn to draw, paint trees from this systematic, lucid instruction book. Copiously illustrated with the author's own sketches, diagrams, and 50 paintings from the early Renaissance to today, it covers composition; structure of twigs, boughs, buds, branch systems; outline forms of major species; how leaf is set on twig; flowers and fruit and their arrangement; etc. 500 illustrations. Bibliography. Indexes. 347pp. 5⅜ x 8.
T1016 Clothbound **$4.50**

HOW PLANTS GET THEIR NAMES, L. H. Bailey. In this basic introduction to botanical nomenclature, a famed expert on plants and plant life reveals the confusion that can result from misleading common names of plants and points out the fun and advantage of using a sound, scientific approach. Covers every aspect of the subject, including an historical survey beginning before Linnaeus systematized nomenclature, the literal meaning of scores of Latin names, their English equivalents, etc. Enthusiastically written and easy to follow, this handbook for gardeners, amateur horticulturalists, and beginning botany students is knowledgeable, accurate and useful. 11 illustrations. Lists of Latin, English botanical names. 192pp. 5⅜ x 8½. T796 Paperbound **$1.15**

PIERRE CURIE, Marie Curie. Nobel Prize winner creates a memorable portrait of her equally famous husband in a fine scientific biography. Recounting his childhood, his haphazard education, and his experimental research (with his brother) in the physics of crystals, Mme. Curie brings to life the strong, determined personality of a great scientist at work and discusses, in clear, straightforward terms, her husband's and her own work with radium and radioactivity. A great book about two very great founders of modern science. Includes Mme. Curie's autobiographical notes. Translated by Charlotte and Vernon Kellogg. viii + 120pp. 5⅜ x 8½. T199 Paperbound **$1.00**

STYLES IN PAINTING: A Comparative Study, Paul Zucker. Professor of Art History at Cooper Union presents an important work of art-understanding that will guide you to a fuller, deeper appreciation of masterpieces of art and at the same time add to your understanding of how they fit into the evolution of style from the earliest times to this century. Discusses general principles of historical method and aesthetics, history of styles, then illustrates with more than 230 great paintings organized by subject matter so you can see at a glance how styles have changed through the centuries. 236 beautiful halftones. xiv + 338pp. 5⅝ x 8½. T760 Paperbound **$2.00**

NEW VARIORUM EDITION OF SHAKESPEARE

One of the monumental feats of Shakespeare scholarship is the famous New Variorum edition, containing full texts of the plays together with an entire reference library worth of historical and critical information: all the variant readings that appear in the quartos and folios; annotations by leading scholars from the earliest days of Shakespeare criticism to the date of publication; essays on meaning, background, productions by Johnson, Addison, Fielding, Lessing, Hazlitt, Coleridge, Ulrici, Swinburne, and other major Shakespeare critics; original sources of Shakespeare's inspiration. For the first time, this definitive edition of Shakespeare's plays, each printed in a separate volume, will be available in inexpensive editions to scholars, to teachers and students, and to every lover of Shakespeare and fine literature. Now ready:

KING LEAR, edited by Horace Howard Furness. Bibliography. List of editions collated in notes. viii + 503pp. 5⅜ x 8½. T1000 Paperbound **$2.25**

MACBETH, edited by Horace Howard Furness Jr. Bibliography. List of editions collated in notes. xvi + 562pp. 5⅜ x 8½. T1001 Paperbound **$2.25**

ROMEO AND JULIET, edited by Horace Howard Furness. Bibliography. List of editions collated in notes. xxvi + 480pp. 5⅜ x 8½. T1002 Paperbound **$2.25**

OTTHELLO, edited by Horace Howard Furness. Bibliography. List of editions collated in notes. x + 471pp. 5⅜ x 8½. T1003 Paperbound **$2.25**

HAMLET, edited by Horace Howard Furness. Bibliography. List of editions collated in notes. Total of 926pp. 5⅜ x 8½. T1004-1005 Two volume set, Paperbound **$4.50**

THE GARDENER'S YEAR, Karel Capek. The author of this refreshingly funny book is probably best known in U. S. as the author of "R. U. R.," a biting satire on the machine age. Here, his satiric genius finds expression in a wholly different vein: a warm, witty chronicle of the joys and trials of the amateur gardener as he watches over his plants, his soil and the weather from January to December. 59 drawings by Joseph Capek add an important second dimension to the fun. "Mr. Capek writes with sympathy, understanding and humor," NEW YORK TIMES. "Will delight the amateur gardener, and indeed everyone else," SATURDAY REVIEW. Translated by M. and R. Weatherall. 59 illustrations. 159pp. 4½ x 6½. T1014 Paperbound **$1.00**

THE ADVANCE OF THE FUNGI, E. C. Large. The dramatic story of the battle against fungi, from the year the potato blight hit Europe (1845) to 1940, and of men who fought and won it: Pasteur, Anton de Bary, Tulasne, Berkeley, Woronin, Jensen, many others. Combines remarkable grasp of facts and their significance with skill to write dramatic, exciting prose. "Philosophically witty, fundamentally thoughtful, always mature," NEW YORK HERALD TRIBUNE. "Highly entertaining, intelligent, penetrating," NEW YORKER. Bibliography. 64 illustrations. 6 full-page plates. 488pp. 5⅜ x 8½. T437 Paperbound **$2.25**

THE PAINTER'S METHODS AND MATERIALS, A. P. Laurie. Adviser to the British Royal Academy discusses the ills that paint is heir to and the methods most likely to counteract them. Examining 48 masterpieces by Fra Lippo Lippi, Millais, Boucher, Rembrandt, Romney, Van Eyck, Velazquez, Michaelangelo, Botticelli, Frans Hals, Turner, and others, he tries to discover how special and unique effects were achieved. Not conjectural information, but certain and authoritative. Beautiful, sharp reproductions, plus textual illustrations of apparatus and the results of experiments with pigments and media. 63 illustrations and diagrams. Index. 250pp. 5⅜ x 8. T1019 Clothbound **$3.75**

GEOMETRY OF FOUR DIMENSIONS, H. P. Manning. Unique in English as a clear, concise intro-duction to this fascinating subject. Treatment is primarily synthetic and Euclidean, although hyperplanes and hyperspheres at infinity are considered by non-Euclidean forms. Historical introduction and foundations of 4-dimensional geometry; perpendicularity; simple angles; angles of planes; higher order; symmetry; order, motion; hyperpyramids, hypercones, hyper-spheres; figures with parallel elements; volume, hypervolume in space; regular polyhedroids. Glossary of terms. 74 illustrations. ix + 348pp. 5⅜ x 8.   S182 Paperbound **$2.00**

PAPER FOLDING FOR BEGINNERS, W. D. Murray and F. J. Rigney. A delightful introduction to the varied and entertaining Japanese art of origami (paper folding), with a full, crystal-clear text that anticipates every difficulty; over 275 clearly labeled diagrams of all important stages in creation. You get results at each stage, since complex figures are logically developed from simpler ones. 43 different pieces are explained: sailboats, frogs, roosters, etc. 6 photographic plates. 279 diagrams. 95pp. 5⅝ x 8⅜.   T713 Paperbound **$1.00**

SATELLITES AND SCIENTIFIC RESEARCH, D. King-Hele. An up-to-the-minute non-technical ac-count of the man-made satellites and the discoveries they have yielded up to September of 1961. Brings together information hitherto published only in hard-to-get scientific journals. In-cludes the life history of a typical satellite, methods of tracking, new information on the shape of the earth, zones of radiation, etc. Over 60 diagrams and 6 photographs. Mathemati-cal appendix. Bibliography of over 100 items. Index. xii + 180pp. 5⅜ x 8½.   T703 Paperbound **$2.00**

LOUIS PASTEUR, S. J. Holmes. A brief, very clear, and warmly understanding biography of the great French scientist by a former Professor of Zoology in the University of California. Traces his home life, the fortunate effects of his education, his early researches and first theses, and his constant struggle with superstition and institutionalism in his work on microorganisms, fermentation, anthrax, rabies, etc. New preface by the author. 159pp. 5⅜ x 8.   T197 Paperbound **$1.00**

THE ENJOYMENT OF CHESS PROBLEMS, K. S. Howard. A classic treatise on this minor art by an internationally recognized authority that gives a basic knowledge of terms and themes for the everyday chess player as well as the problem fan: 7 chapters on the two-mover; 7 more on 3- and 4-move problems; a chapter on selfmates; and much more. "The most important one-volume contribution originating solely in the U.S.A.," Alain White. 200 diagrams. Index. Solutions, viii + 212pp. 5⅜ x 8.   T742 Paperbound **$1.25**

SAM LOYD AND HIS CHESS PROBLEMS, Alain C. White. Loyd was (for all practical purposes) the father of the American chess problem and his protégé and successor presents here the diamonds of his production, chess problems embodying a whimsy and bizarre fancy entirely unique. More than 725 in all, ranging from two-move to extremely elaborate five-movers, including Loyd's contributions to chess oddities—problems in which pieces are arranged to form initials, figures, other by-paths of chess problem found nowhere else. Classified accord-ing to major concept, with full text analyzing problems, containing selections from Loyd's own writings. A classic to challenge your ingenuity, increase your skill. Corrected republica-tion of 1913 edition. Over 750 diagrams and illustrations. 744 problems with solutions. 471pp. 5⅜ x 8½.   T928 Paperbound **$2.25**

FABLES IN SLANG & MORE FABLES IN SLANG, George Ade. 2 complete books of major American humorist in pungent colloquial tradition of Twain, Billings. 1st reprinting in over 30 years includes "The Two Mandolin Players and the Willing Performer," "The Base Ball Fan Who Took the Only Known Cure," "The Slim Girl Who Tried to Keep a Date that was Never Made," 42 other tales of eccentric, perverse, but always funny characters. "Touch of genius," H. L. Mencken. New introduction by E. F. Bleiler. 86 illus. 208pp. 5⅜ x 8.   T533 Paperbound **$1.00**

Prices subject to change without notice.

Dover publishes books on art, music, philosophy, literature, languages, history, social sciences, psychology, handcrafts, orientalia, puzzles and entertainments, chess, pets and gardens, books explaining science, intermediate and higher mathematics, math-ematical physics, engineering, biological sciences, earth sciences, classics of science, etc. Write to:

Dept. catrr.
Dover Publications, Inc.
180 Varick Street, N.Y. 14, N.Y.